Beauty
OF MORALITY
VOLUME 3

Beauty

OF MORALITY

VOLUME 3

PIERRE EDENS SULLY

Rev. date: 12/07/2016

To order additional copies of this book, contact:
Xlibris
1-888-795-4274
www.Xlibris.com
Orders@Xlibris.com
749687

CONTENTS

INTRODUCTION

I am a man quite cool and calm, incapable of feeling other things than the poetry, live and breathe only for the poetry, have a heart, of eyes and of ears only for the poetry. I am perhaps considered as a poet the purest and the most correct among the poets.

Dear reader, would you talk about the greatest talent that I deployed in the city of Brooklyn? This easy move, these harmonious verses, this character sometimes flat and sometimes gay, brilliant, pathetic, loving, somber and always elevated, where the readers are not shocked, even in the transitions the hardest that they were well-prepared and resolved! This exact precision where you cannot either remove or augment, where all are done!__ The quality of those harmonies so well-distributed and so well-adapted, without bothering the charming part that I have always seen as the principal, always noble!

O reader! I prove that you have much intelligence! I give you an infinite price at all critics that you will bring out, at all what you do. The things the simplest and the most ordinary, in passing by your mouth, become sublime. This book shades with some colorful reflects, without a style the most insignificant and the most common, it suddenly acquires the sacred characters of the beauty, of the inspiration, of the genius. Specially, I respect it, I put in relief your spirit. The vogue is there for welcoming it, for setting it off to advantage. How do you believe that a poet who wrote wonderfully the poetry, who is smart and who is poor, ahead who nobody sides with, can have the intelligence? This book must be the most admired, the most applauded, the most sought-after, the best savored, it is one that manifests as the fire of holy Spirit.

I am going to praise a great poet who is Mr Walt Whitman, at the view of honors rendered back at the memory of this great master, a poet who felt his soul exalted, grown, taking a run up to the sky with immortal shadow. I would like to bring back all his sublime poems that seemed being written only for the angels, his sublime potries that were with their parts quite suave, moving, harmonious, full of enthusiasm, full of irresistible effects as he tended to make them so splendid under his powerful pen. What an ardent and passionate soul, what a soul completely human, the readers felt to stir under his poetic forms that knew the limits only these ones of the infinite.

I will finish his eulogy, weak homage from me, but very well-merited. O reader, will not you tell that the death took him away too early, that with a talent so transcendant, he was bor for having a fate more gratified, and that he was merited of being more known, more thorough. Whaterver they accuse me of particularity, neither of flattering, nobody courts the dead persons. What I have advanced, I feel it, I have always felt it, and he left to the time and to the connaisseurs or experts the care of appreciating the sublime productions that left for us.

In United States, are there enough marvels for making us forget our immortal stay? Enough brilliant concerts for charming our ears? At last for our good turns, is there enough love? Are not we the example, as well as the torch? Are not we the light enlightening the world?

By learning from the mouths of all those who are near me, and whose the praises, as a pure and hidden spring, did not dry up on the august poet that you have pointed out; by learning from the mouths full of love, of respect, of gratitude, how I have just guessed by reading on noble and grave physionmies many admirable versesof virtue, of beneficence, of generosity, of touching actions and of sublime traoits,___ my heart looks at them as the best details with respect, with admiration, with love.

No 1

Gall and wormwood

I

What a criminal indifference! All imams, preachers
Recognized the vanity of their rude science,
Of their methods, of their systems, of their lectures.
They go until to their mistakes, their intense
Lies; they go until to
Conclude this capital
Confession: "Those undue
Libraries being little1
Pretended as treasure of sublime knowledges,
Are only a humiliating storehouse
Of contradictions and of mistakes," and they please
To set on fire in the libraries like a mouse!

II

They confess necessity of reviewing more
Our ideas at their origin, of remarking
The human consciousness, of forgetting encore
All what they have learned; and nobody is putting
Himself at the work! Whence
They plunge us in the deep
Abyss where their ignorance
Drove us as the stupid.
What! Moralists, diplomats, divine messengers!
You do not see souls the purest and noblest, the most

1

In love with fairness and beauty, the natures
The most beautiful, the most vigorous, almost
Sagging suddenly, pining
Away, wasting away
With the pains and dying
So desperate one day
Of not meeting at each step, in our society
Quite well-constructed, only the iniquities
And madness! You call yourselves the mercenary
Victims of civilization and centuries!

III

For you see with reason in individuals
Quite civilized and moralized only a monster
Of perversity! What! From your codes of morals
And of philosophy you see only hungrier
Legions, slaves of a penny
And ready at all crimes
For escaping poverty!
Nevertheless, sometimes,
In your society of hell, the millions poor
Human creatures,__ children of God like you, and then
A blood also pure than yours, a heart often more
Solemn and noblest, millions of poor human
Creatures also honest
And hard-working cannot
Find back from their busiest
Work a nice lodging flat2,
Some warm clothes, sufficient meals, certain days of rest.
The millions poor young women have only the choice
Between a homicidal misery and oldest...........3,
And so many young people then cannot rejoice.

IV

What you see by experience of fifty
Centuries how much the reason of human being
Is unpowerful against his/ her passion! See,
You persist despite that in your upsetting
Errors, sources of all
Wrongs and of all crimes! And
You continue to haul
From top of your widened
Pulpits quite well-kept at great expense, your supernal4
Aspersions! By a blind attachment to your crazy
Theories quite political, metaphysical;
You reject obstinately all good policy
Of regeneration that
Is not yours!__ Furthermore,
You turn aside the fat
Heads scornfully encore
To the unique name of the man who thus found, __ what
You would truly search, what you do not understand
Yet, o reiterators, ___ who found the plot
To gain practice of truth wit bloom of passions, no end;

V

O holy performers! You who steal from nature
Its secret the most precious, who unveil again
Laws of social mechanism, who discover
For the humankind a path of bliss quite so certain,
And a fixed compass for
Guiding us in that way
Of salvation traced encore
By Holy Being Each day,
Who tend to discover with care the theories
Of attraction! Ah, you shudder with anger

By that word, you fume with rage by those memories
Of the man who carried out the light in your bigger
Darkness, who helped you see
Your ignorance, your dense
Ineptitude, who truly
Stripped your eloquence,
Who made you feel your absurdities, who put clear
The falsity of your pompous doctrines! You pursue
Only with furor your enormous babel of square
Sophism, of fallacy; you bring nothing new.

VI

You daily add a new standard as established
At that monument of your prides and your follies,
You believe to find a shelter against a punished
Deluge! Be careful! The wave is so calm, it is
Patient, it waits; further
It does not make even
Listen a light murmur,
Even a move again;
But be careful! If it is revolted by,
If it is entered suddenly into furor,
If it jumps over its limit, alas! Your high
Games are up; nothing will spare you, this is its anger.
You see pitilessly
All days of million poor
Human creatures truly
Die of despair encore!
Be careful! When the people, thanks to this light
That penetratedin them and warmed them more by more,
Will be able to plan, to know where they are quite;
When they will be able to tell with a heart so poor:

VII

"We are brothers. What! This blood whose my hand is tinted
Is the blood of my brother! And in what purpose,
In what interest did I kill my brother so wrll-bred?
Ah! Traitors who told me that he was my morose
And mortal enemy
And who directed my
Arm in the darkness. See,
The bigands who then fly!
See, the assassins! The day where the people will
Be hit by remorses and by that idea,
For that day, unhappiness to you! Then your real
Last hour will sound. For that day is not truly
Farther than you believe
It. Do not see the things
Cannot thus go or leave
Longtime in these standings?
Do not you see that such a situation is so
Intolerable? Ah! You will worry about
Your amusements, about your deplorable and flow
Indifference, about your meaness, without doubt.

VIII

Then the happy men of the world will have certain
Terrible count to ask you, and this is you who
At this time guide us, who would be able to then
Assure the welfare of workers and a new
Quietude of healthy
Persons without moment
Of truth, without fury,
Without sudden moment.
It is very horrible to see when every
Religion shakes the hands with the corruption and

Criminality; but where worshipers truly
Could escape or hide themselves; no one is quite so bland.
1-little is an adverb. 2-flat means apartment.3- the dots of
suspension replace profession and the expression "oldest
profession" means prostitution.4- supernal means holy.

No 2

Heaviness of heart

I

O my brothers and my sisters!
I am talking to you and to
Myself with all the good manners.
We did not think that we have a new
Crime to reproach us. Our conscience
Cries to us however this is then
The truth. And we shed tears! Whence
We shed tears of shame, of burden
Of heart! We are right to weep; for
If we could think without worry
About several children encore
Dying by our fault and apathy.

II

It does not suffice to weep or
To lament on a past mending1
Loss. All our sobs and all our more
Tears will not give back anything
Or the life to dying children.
What we must do, this is a set2
Aim changing us, not to then
Fall again in same faults as debt

III

What we must do, this is to honor,
To esteem the life of others,
Specially journalists, author,
Artists, actors, poets, writers
From their lifetimes as their deaths,
Not to suffer that such poets
Die of poverty without breaths3,
Not to permit the tomfoolish4 threats
As those who animated and
Cruelly hurt the soul truly
Noble and tender of the grand
Poets that you let dieof worry.

IV

Yes, my reader, a firm purpose
Of becoming wise, reasoning
To give up all many morose
Critics that the art of writing
Leads to nothing. The unique way
Is to form your tastes and your judgments,
To learn to reason just today,
To give up the huge arguments.

V

Did not you stay with the upset
Dispositions of my mind, to
The dark melancholy that yet
Seized the ardent soul, and who
Let me tell as told Chenier:
"Tired by the scorn of fools, I turn
My own eyes through the sepulcher."
I stop me, my reader so stern,

By fear of exciting too much
Painfully the extreme feeling
Whose you indeed displayed to the such
Representations of striking 5

VI

I throw a veil on this painting
Too sad, too lugubrious, too bitter
For your hearts, o my discerning
Readers, you promised me moreover
To be fairer in the share
Of your graces, of your favors,
Of your praises. Let God quite fair
Keep you going on such humors.

1-past mending means irreparable.2-set means fixed, firm. 3-breaths means complaints, murmurs in the improper sense. 4-tomfoolish means ridiculous. 5-the dots of suspension replace writers.

No 3

Verve

—※—

I

This is too bad that I cannot
Tell you with a voice so lively
How beautiful you are a lot,
Specially about this beauty
That the brilliance of soul does make
On the face. O celestial light!
How much you would have a wide lake
Of joy to spread in my sad night!

II

If you knew how sad and somber
Is my life, __ so much you would
Have beautiful soul and better
Heart quite well-placed! Noble and good
Woman! O poor woman! Your unique
Historian is not the whole
In some two words! The authentic
Thoughts for you are never so droll.

III

The veritable verve, this is
The sensibility of soul,
Exalted by the great ideas,

By view of noble and of sole
Deciding match, specially
By spectacle of humankinds.
The stimulants naturally
Excite the sensesand the minds.

IV

The stimulants do not exalt
The soul or the thought. No,
The enthusiasm and salt1
Are not a stuff that is apropos
Given or that is removed at
Will; this is the infinite fire
That burns the great soul and that
Makes poet a hero quite higher.
Salt means vigor.

No 4

Pillar of power

I

Ah! I really do not fancy1
To the magnetism. Therefore,
If this force of attraction truly
Existed in the body encore2,
How could you, but unique of so
Strong desires, how could you so calmly
Follow your inspiration? Oh!
You would be lifted up like a bee
From your seat; and then I woud see
You flying from a bush to other,
Based on most or least gravity
Of each one, here and there gather
Some kisses so high-flown, deeper.

II

You who then feel as if you are
The god, the sovereign, the master;
You feel as if are the pillar
Of power to put all a utter
Capital, all a population,
All a heart in a nervous
Excitement or agitation!
You indeed claim to be thus
The king, today the queen, today

The prince, the princess the most proud,
The ladies the fullest of the day
Or the most stylish and so loud3,
These things for me, for me only,
Nothing rather than to listen
Me. To sense that you are the shiny
Star around which a world does then
Gravitates! What a joy! What a glory!

III

Verily, God is my witness
If I knew what praise to indicate
To those that you listen unless
Everyday, I bustle to create
It at your eyes in all its ray;
For if I envy you something,
This is not your outstanding sway
Or your renown, your long-lasting
Fortune, your bliss, that I wish for
To see improving endlessly
On the contrary if it is more
Possible; what I then envy
From you, this is the so intense
Power that the nature gave you
To do what is well, as you, whence
I feel some praise cannot too
Match for a heart quite generous
And noble the blessing for one
Of thesepoor guys for whom your muse
Is an angel ahead your own
Glory, ahead your financial
Sovereign, I regret absolutely one thing,
This is that, whereas the racial
Fortune, just only concerning3

You, strew your way with the flowers,
It leaves the misery in use
Of hollowing out the bowers5
Of poor people being your cues
Or your brothers who6 meanwhile,
You have a soul to understand
Them better than any body, while
Have same sights with you as grand.

IV

I attended an excited
Triumph of Odette. Moreover,
You you would have as me the extended
Admiration, if you could further
See again one more time this grace
And this personified verses.
And you will have smiled with a trace
Of pleasure to see with ease
The setting filling up to
Flowers at severaltimes. A true
Harvest of flowers, on the price
Of exaggeration. And too,
The remarkable time that Odette
Needs for picking them up has been
For all the spectators a set7
Continuation of serene
Enjoyment. How many divine
Smiles, ineffable kisses, sweet
Thanks from heart, expressed by a fine
And charming gesture, did she transmit
With her hand of goddess, flower
Among the flowers, to gather
Flowers that did not stop with power
Pouring on her from all nicer

Boxes, without counting presidential
Box. If I was a painter, what
Entrencing paint! What essential
Enthusiasm at her pat
Coping! In all the galleries,
All the bushes have smiled with cheer,
All the whole physiognomies
Were bright, all the hands clapped, no beer.
1 fancymeans believe in the improper sense. 2-encore is an
adverb of quantity and mens again.3- loud mens extravagant
in the improper sense.4- concerning means toward, apropos.
5- bowers means cabin, house 6- who meanwhile, who
being a relative pronoun of brothers is the subject of verb
have. 7-set is a qualificative adjective of continuation

No 5

Moral defect

I

The poverty is not only
Felt as a lack, it is also
A moral defect. We really
Feel the need to repeat apropos
That the poverty is not vice;
It does not let itself being
A shameful vice where the precise
Fortune, at the corresponding
Or same titlethan the nobles,
Is respected as a value
Than only the birth unless
Should give certain persons the view.

II

In such a way for succeeding,
The best way, this is to be a fool.
The world is only full of daring
Fools; what a regard can man full
Of spirit show in the world? And
As long as the virtue and wit1
Without the money is in hand
As useless furniture. Be lit2,
Be old, be ugly, be stupid,
Have money, all doors open for you,

Everybody will court you, will need
You. You will be forgiven too.

III

I invite you to mull over3
This word the most enthralling
That the heart of a man ever
Struck, this word the most engaging
Than all the books that we should read
In golden letters on the cave,
To the foot of this splendid
Statue of white marble so grave
In which illustrious sculptor
Saved us the divine attributes
Of that creatire truly super4:
And why are we, as the tributes,
Unless for making allowance
Of our fortunes to the poor men?
Why did God truly countenance5
That there among the human
Beings, who are all brothers,
The rich and the poor, otherwise
So that the ones adjust to old-timers6
A merit of their richness in rise,
And others of their poverty?

IV

To be noble and to be great,
This is to havethe soul enough7
Of compassiuon and of straight
Devotion, this is to have in tough
Horror the egoism, pride,
Avarice; this is to do good

As log you can; this is to confide8
His fortune, his life, for saving
His brothers; this is to love truths
And justice; this is defending,
Honoring, protecting the youths,
The virtue, the work and talent;
This to appreciate value
And to know to compliment
And to recompense; this is to
Appear prouder of the esteem
Of a people than of the faith
And homage of thousand extreme
And rich countrymenquite so rathe9;
This is to like to spread the light
Among these ones, in order not
To find oneself honored by right
Men, not by brutes as idiot.
1-wit means intelligence, brain, mind. 2-lit means drunk,
intoxicated. 3-mull over means meditate. 4-super means
wonderful. 5-coumtenance means allow, permit. 6-old-timers
means old people in the improper sense. 7-enough means full.
8confide mens disclose reveal impart.. 9 rathe means mature.

No 6

You who take away my heart and my soul! The good news that I received about you threw me in a frenzy. Since at that time, my thoughts turned on you, and you made me become poet without knowing you; and then the earth became for me a place where the words were born from silence; a place where the beatings of heart did not cease; a place where I listened the leaves and the birds sung your beauty; a place where each person sculpted your picture in my heart.

The first day that I saw you, my soul quickly received you, and then I drunk the poison that know infects my senses and my reason. Your nice eyes, your character, your sweet words and all that are in you developed in me a love for you.

I love you so much, mortal start of my heart! When I was deep in the prayer, my faith were crammedby the thought of you. You are the first woman who injects the tender liquid of love in the filter of my heart. Our both hearts have the same dimension as if God seemed to create us the one for the other. Dear Odette, by what charm have you come to distract mr? the voice that has called your name is sweeter than the night that asleeps, more gracious than the voice of anangel. You are the consolatory of my heart. I would never miss to see so many arts in your behavior, and while I find in it a gentleness and a honor. Joy of my spirit, tender like the grass, charming like the flower! The inimaginable, the unknown__ this is what you give me to my soul since oit follows your direction. At last, obtain that the integral reward of your bliss comes back to you. Restore your imprudence and permit that your heart fills up neither

to look for finding again the past, but love. Catch at each
inatant the unalike newness and do not prepare your own
joy. Know that in this fine place, a joy will surprise you.
How seet it is to live in you! I find you again with delight in
the fruits and in the flowers. You made my life so interesting
and formidable. I cannot imagine how solitary I would be
without you. I thank God that he blessed our resolution by
making appear the best in each of us. I donot miss to say that
you make out the best in me and I want to past the rest of my
life for giving you the attention and for recomforting you.
I hope you will see how devoted I will be as a husband,
how concerned I will be in providing the best
experience and opportunities for our family.
In this sumptuous place, I welcome you with a deep emotion,
and I give you the sincere assurance that our matrimonial
union will never be fallenin ruin. I belong to you more than
myself. I wishyou have my soul, my heart, and my words.

Good fellow

I

Let you beging by making you
Forgive, by dint of nobleness
And of greatness, as a true
Result of amazing deeds, natheless1
This title of preachers is not
Dishonored by so many base
Acts, by so many heinous, flat
Crimes. Invite, if you can, in your place
A true american diplomat.
Try hard to equal him in braveness,
In distinction, in reverence,
In talents, in unboastfulness2,
In lights, and in beneficence.
It is useless to keep on telling
The ancient things that God will come
To change the world, or God during
Can change all the things at random3.

II

Try hard to love the people,
To encourage them, to favor
Them, to honor them, to cuddle4
Them; try hard to acquaint and tutor
Them with genius, with talent,

With work; to be fair, clemency,
The source of caring is patent
And is perceived outside you truly.

III

Be foolish, be ridiculous.
This is the only way to make
You delicious, unportentous,
Unique to the eyes of the wake
Crowd, especially to the eyes
Of honorable. More you will
Tell some follies, some routine lies,
Some extravagances, some real
Impertinances, more you then
Will appear sublime to them.
There are only foolish and broken
Heads who please, who charm, who attract them;
There is only this that5 they like, that6 they admire,
That7 they pay, only this alike
Kind of men who entertain as fire,
Who make laugh. Happy are those who
Are crazy, they possess the earth.
The courtiers must have neither
Honor for succeeding with the mirth.

IV

Drinking the delicious wine,
Eating the exquisite meal, possess
Pretty women, sleeping on a fine
And soft bed, thereis the flawless
Wisdom. All leftovers are only
Vanity. To love our fellow
Creatures? Vanity! To study8

Duties that religion apropos
Imposes? Vanity! All is
Only vanity! And living,
This is possessing, this is
Enjoying, this is obtaining
To our balance a multitude
Of low sycophants and of flat
Jokesters who go into a crude
Rapture over all we let cat9
Out of the bag, and who chasten
As it suits the man of genius
Who importune us. I even
Do not know them for brave men thus.

1-natheless means nevertheless,. 2-unboastfulness means modesty. 3-at random means aimlessly, purposelessly.4- cuddle means appreciate. 5-this that they like, that being a relative pronoun of this is the complement of direct object of verb like. 6- that run after, that being a relative pronoun of this is the complement of direct object of verb run. 7- that they admire. That being a telative pronoun of this is the complement of direct object of verb admire.. 8- study means practice. 9- let cat out of bag is an expression that means tell.

No 8

Heavenly land

I

I admire highly american people. Then
United States
Transport me, lift me above myself, broaden
My nice debates,
Open up my soul and my heart, make me appear
At my proper
Eyes higher than ten feet, but in the feelings so fair
That it ever
Inspires me, in the transports that it spurs1 in me;
There is something
Sad and painful, that makes me find my own country
Unpromising
And drop me in some aspirations so puzzling
In the desires
Quite vague and inexpressible, and while nothing
On-earth, one hires2,
Cannot satisfy. In this country, the dance,
Music and song
Amuse me, distract me, excite me like a dense
Wine quite strong
Of California, astound me deliciously,
At last give me
Only the joy and the pleasure, without any
Great lethany,

Without any melancholy, in such a way
That, without sharing
The ridiculous complex of crown for the play
Of Lion King
And others, in putting them so high in my heart
Or my esteem,
I applaud them with all my heart; as my large part,
I like to scream
With a great joy to join them voluntarily
To ovations
Whose they are the object. All are naturally
My adorations.

II

My ambition is at last satisfied. Indeed,
The bliss does not
Remain only in the wealths or in the candid
Splendor or flat;
It is entirely in our heart. Let us applaud
America!
It carry everything in it, if we then laud
To drink it, ah,
The cup of the rapture. The rapture, this nectar
Makes the sweetest
Stuffs, comes from the one of flowers newly so far
Hatched to the best
Side of the rivers, of rays of sun, of murmurs
Of waters,
Of perfumes of breeze, and of song of birds; one stirs
And one ponders.
America smiles at the nature, the trees thus
Crown with flowers
And greens movebackward and forward by the dexterous
Blows or twisters.

O my friends! Come to err with me on american
Sands, on grasses
In bloom; come together to the pure spring to then
Quench thirsts, wishes
Of our bosoms just as we find the lost rapture.
There is no room
For doubt and uncertainty today, the nature
Isquite in bloom.
1-spurs means excites. 2- hires means gets,
lets out in the improper sense.

No 9

Brotherhood

I

Why do the pride, the power, the honor,
The prestige, the raceand class, skin color
Put the hardness in the heart of those who
Are eager to maintain them in our due
World? And before requiring from others
The brotherly life, with some good manners,
I begun by practicing it at such
Point that I naturally deserve much
The title of universal brother.
Let us walk in this nice way together!

!!

I never like to class human beings
In different categories, groupings
Having more or less right to my pure love.
I situate me toward all, right of1 _____
Even toward menwho have no reason
In a brotherly link at any season.
Feelings so ingenerate2 of my heart
Are enough to make me fraternal in part
For all creature. Do not surprise to see
In thetorment of others, I really
Become more the brother of men. Secret
Of my conduct is very simple, yet

I refuse to see in all men other
Things than brother who ties us together.

III

Thus considered, men the most dishonest
Could become fraternal. If all modest
People appreciate me, those are not
They feel that I raise on them a pot
Of looks that procure no condemnation
But love, a fraternal contemplation3. I believe
In them. Because I am so objective
And good, I think normally that the spring
Of bounty is not dry and undamping
In the others who feel themselvesloved thuws
And start to love at their run withoiut fuss4.

IV

I always treat others with a bounty,
With a sweetness, with a great charity
Quite indicible, but only because
I softened, crushed, prostrated any cause
Of hardness in me; because I then watch
With an implacable rigor the catch5
Movements of my hand and my tongue, and
The lighting of my eyes. I am a grand
Dictator of iron, a violent,
A tyrant for all the so jubilant
Appetites of my nature. This is grace
To this inside order and inner case6
That I can drive me on the other
Beings without trampling on them ever.

V

Then I am capable of acquaintaing
Me fraternally with all the living
Souls and things, of worming my way into
Them, in the corners the darkest and too
The most isolated, but uniquely
Because I am quite so previously
Humiliated, mortified until
The perfect neglect of myself. By will,
I can smile enthusiastically
And purely, but because I am happy
Of all and without need for my person;
Because I really try not to worsen
Me; because I do not want anything
Of those things that provoke the bickering.

VI

I knew to see and to taste numerous
Beauties of earth, but as soon as I thus
Ignored them, so I left them far behind
Me; where I know superior and kind
Realities to those ones that people
Can offer. I won innumerable
Human hearts; I received as offering
Some enormous treasuresof living
Human amour, but uniquely because
I am with all the people without pause.

VII

From the interior of ourselves and
From the exterior, we are opened
To receive many messages, orders
Quite negative that use us. Some masters

Give us a good point and we become strong.
Nevertheless everyone needs among
Nice words to try to find some important
Words of encouragement or inducement
To say someone, provided that this be
True or to say him that he earns bonny
Ressources___ what is always true; this is
A great act of charity or bounties.
Why? Because our need of being welcomed,
Esteemed is constant, even whenovercomed7.

VIII

The virtue of humility is to
Accept each other such one is, too
To accept that one tells us that. Virtue
Of charity is not to please oneself to
Underline the defectsof others. Then
Help others to see clear, to be strong often,
In order to void to themselves the feeling
Quite depressing, later of not telling
The yes or the no that it should not be.
When someone procures a delinquency
That surprises you, that irritates you,
Do not try to go to judge him quickly, too
You have to try to go positively
In his inside motivations truly.

IX

Forgiveness is the unique way to peace
And gladness. My grand-mother did not miss
To teach me love, respect for everyone,
Taught me not to see everything or one
Thing in life along racial line. All are

The same. Hatred is more than a bizarre
Negative outlook. It is a destructive
And self-destructive power that we live.
Why does everybody run after you
And why do they have the desire to view8
You, to listen you, and to just submit
To you? About your trait, you are not a sweet
And handsome man, you have no great science,
You are not noble, but only good sense.

X

Where does this come from that everybody
Run after you? You need know why to me,
Everybody runs after you? I keep
That from my grand-mother quite very deep
Who contemplated the evil and good;
For my eyes never saw among the rude
And cursed persons who had been the vilest,
The most insufficient, and the greatest
Devil than me; and as for doing
The wonderful work that I am owing
To do, the mother- naturedid not find
On the earth the vilest and quite unkind
Creature than me, she has just chosen
Me for confusing the noble men.

1-right of means at once. 2-ingenerate means natural- born. 3-
contemplation means look in the improper sense. 4- fuss means
trouble. 5- catch uses as a qualificative adjective of movements
and means discovered in the improper sense. 6- case means state.
7- overcomed = even when we are overcomed. 8- view means see.

No 10

Maladjustment of religion

I

Scandal of religion in world is its secular
Element such as its prestige as a social
Institution, its power is a political
Agency, its endowment as an official
Foster-child of nation or class so pratical.
It identifies itself so intimately
With capitalism and with the tenet
Of individualism. The jeopardy
Of religion lies in a skill2 to adjust yet
Itself to national ways3 than to spurn4 them on a par.

II

The religionism is only a play of mind
And an idea that is similar to image
Of an ideal state given by Plato is
Considered here as utopia or usage.
Christians feigned that they can be glad in poverties,
And can be insensible to all the insults,
To ingratitude, to losses of properties,
As to those ones of parents and friends and adults,
Can only consider death as a thing or ease
Quite fair that must cheer or grieve, either to mind;

III

Whence they feigned that they cannot be conquered either
By the pleasure or pain, can feel the iron or
Fire in some part of their bodies without even
Pushing the least sigh, neither throw an only more
Tear. This phantom of virtue and constancy then
Imagined6 plesaed them by calling themselves flawless,
Or Christian. They left to man all faults that they found
In him, and have almost raised none of their weakness.
Instead of making of their vices the profound
And frightful drawsthat served to correct further,

IV

They7 traced to man the idea of a perfection
And of a heroism whose he8 is not so
Capable and urged him impossible. Hi!
Thus the wise9, who is not, or who is apropos
Only imaginary, finds himself and by
Himself above all events and all harms; either
The drop the most painful, either hurt the sharpest
Could not wheedle a plaint from them; sky and earth ever
Can be upside and down without training them at rest
In their fall, they stayed out of objection.

V

Nevertheless, religious leaders remain firm
On the ruins of the universe. They do not
Demand the souls quite smart, evil and malignant,
But souls who have sweetness and suppleness and that
Last both will never fail in them as important
Because they serve to leaders trap for deceiving
The simple persons and for setting off their real
Artifices. Churchly leadersare desiring

The persons who have a good heart as they at will
Are so possible, easy, obliging for a long-term.

VI

Sometimes it is less true that the evil people
Who thus harm, and good people who thus make suffer.
Such man lived during all his life, laborious,
Sad, ill-conceived, greedy, crawling, subject, tender
And interest; and another man who is thus
Born happy, peaceful, lazy and magnificent,
If a courage quite proud and far of all baseness;
The needs of life, the situation so flagrant10
Where we are, the law of necessity then press,
Urge nature, govern its great changes so total.

VII

Thus such man actually in himself cannot
Define himself: too many things that are really
Outside of him alter him, change him, upset him;
He is not precisely what he is or what truly
He appears to be. Penetrating thoroughly grim
Contrariety of minds, of tastes, and feeling,
I am very more amazed to see that thousand
Men who build a nation are agglomerating
In a same country for speaking a same planned
Language, to live under the same laws as good spot,

VIII

Few only escape them; and as all disgrace can
Happen them, they should be prepatred at all disgrace.
Uncertainty, fear, dejection do not move away;
On the contrary, I only doubt that the grace,
Happiness, smile quite excessive serve anyway

To the men who are mortal. This is toyeld at
The nature and to fear ythe death rather than to
Make continual efforts, to arm with the prat
Reasons and ideas, to be endlessly to true
Grappling with oneself for not fearing them11 often.

IX

By example, nothing is more unbearable
To a person than to be in the fdull rest,
Out of passion, out of belief, out of amusement,
Out of application. He feels since his nearest
Dependence, his doubtfulness, his abandonment,
His scarcity, his heplessness, his emptiness.
So incontinent, he will come from the bottom
Of his soul: ennui, darkness, chagrin, sadness,
Resentment, despair, need, vice. This is the wisdom
Of work that takes them away from us, makes us stable.

X

There are only our duties that cost us, because
Their practice only concerns the things that we are
Straight by obliged to do. Their practice has not been
Followed the great eulogies that are so far
All those that excite to praisable acts quite keen12,
And that13 support us in our enterprises. Whence
The religious leader does not like a pompous
Piety that attracts to himthe intendance
Of the needs of poor people, and that14 makes him thus
Holder oh their patrimony on any cause;

XI

He does not like an ostentacious piety
That makes his house for public depot where happen
Distributions. Who could doubt that he is gentle
Man, if those are not perhaps his creditors. Then
I dare almost assuring that accidental
Men know better to take measures than to follow then
Them, to determine what they must do and what they must
Say than to do or to say what it is often
Suitable. Who would dare promising oneself just
To please the men without a pompous vanity?

XII

Would a pastor, good a powerful he is, want
Undertakeit? He tries, although he gets thus
Accustomed to make an affair by himself from
Their pleasures; he opens his church to his precious
Servitors; he admits them almost in his feedom
And in his intimity; even in his places
Whose the only view is a spectable; he grieves
Them the choice of plays, of concerts, of beverages;
He adds a splendid welcome; he conceives
Them in society with same pastimes or wont.

XIII

The great servitor becomes amiable and
The devotee is familial and human.
Conditions of comedian are infamous
For the three pure persons who are one God, and then
Honorable for the tenebrous angels. Thus
The sky thinks about him as a light and the earth
Sees him as a great performer. The penetration
Of religion, joined at selfishness of priests as worth,

Makes them forget that the reason and invention15
Are in all climates, that one thinks just in each land.
1-tenet means doctrine in the improper sense. 2- skill means
readiness. 3-ways means civilization in the improper sense.4- spurn
means refuse. 6- imagined is an adjective past participe of phantom.
7-they traced, they replaces Christians. 8- he is not so, he repladced
man. 9-wise is the subject of vrerb finds.. 11-flagrant means evident.
12-for not fearing them, them replaces nature and death. 12-keen
means vigorous. 13-and that support, that being a relative pronounof
those is the subject of verb support. 14-and that makes him thus,
that being a relative pronoun of piety. 15- invention means fiction

Godly moralists

I

The spirit of moderation and a certain
Wisdom in the behavior then leave the men
In the obscurity:
They need great virtues for being admired and known,
Or perhaps great vices. Nevertheless, men on
The conduct of wealthy
And poor indifferently, drive themselves to true
Partiality, charmed, seduced by the success too.

II

It is very nearly happened that the blessed crime
Is not praised as the virtue, and the sublime1
Bliss goes not hold virtues.
This is a black assault, this is a dirty and
Odious e might, rather than this one that the grand
Revenues2
Could not justify. In an evil man there
Is nothing for being a great man quite so fair.

III

Eulogize the vies and projects of evil
Moralists; admire his conduct as a devil;
Distend3 his cleverness
In order to use by the means the most proper
And shortest for reaching its end, if its tender
End is bad, cautiousness
Has no part of it, and where cautiousness misses,
We thus find the greatness or the celebrities.

IV

The moralists who condemn the atrocities
Of war get along well with the one who wages
War. Divine man hardly
Hides his joy and his vanity by some outside
Of modesty. There is key of sciences and pride,
Where he naturally
Never goesin; he passes his life to decipher
Philosophy, culture of Middle-East forever,

V

These of Greece and thes ones of Roma. And then
The idioms the most inutile, with certain
Characters the most
Bizarre and the most magical, are precisely
What enlivens his passion and what normally
Excites his work; almost
He complains those who limit themselves cleverly
To know his idioms ads the theology.

Vi

He reads all the stories and ignores the story;
He glances through all the divine looks, and really
Benefit nothing, for
This is in him a sterility of facts and
Of principles that cannot be greater and planned,
But to tell the truth more,
Better harvest and richness the most abundant
Of talks that can invent ideas as his grand slant4.

VII

His memory is overwhelmed, while his mind then
Remains very empty. Therefore the divine man
Is called good arbitrer
In a quarrel of parents or in an issue
Of family, he is in the side of well-to-do,
As if I just prefer
To say for the richest side, and then he is not
Convinced that the one who earns wealths can be wrong a lot.

VIII

If he is well- treated by an opulent man,
To whom he knows how to drceive or maul5 often
Whose he is parasite,
Whose he can have the profit, he does not cajole
His wife, he does not make to her either the droll
Advance or illicit
Declaration; he runs away and leaves to her
His bible; and if he is not also surer
Of her than himself. Thus
He moves away more to laud or seduce her more
By jagon of devotion or prayer. Encore
He knows where are gorgeous

Women the most sociable and the most docile
Than his former friends who are also facile.

IX

He does not leave his former friends for longtime. For
The women who bloom and thrive at the shade of more
Prayers suit him, only
With this little difference that6 he neglects those
Who get old, and that7 he cultivates young as rose,
And between the jolly
Women the most well-shaped; they leave; he leaves; they come
Back, he comes back; they stay, he stays with the wisdom;

X

This is in all places and at all the chsen
Hours that he has consolation to see them. Then
Who could not be edified
About it? They8 are devout, he is a devout. Thus
A devout is not either greedy, or dangerous,
Or unfair, or cold-eyed,
Or even interested; he is not a devout,
But he wants to be such a person very stout,
And by a perfect and high
Imitation, although a false imitation,
He only saves his interest and his donation.
What I think and what I
Call in the world a nice salvation, those are
The decoration often profane, the so rare9
Places often reserved
And prayed, the books often distributed as to
Theater, the interviews and the rendez-vous
Quite frequent and preserved,
The murmurs and the causeries quite very stunning,

Someone gets up on a stand, and he is speaking
Familiarly and
Divinely, without other zeal than to assemble
The people, to amuse them, until an ample
Orchestra or band,
Of voices that concert and harmonize before
Execution. To me, this is to cry out more
Than the zeal of godly
House consumes me, and to draw the light veil that thus
Covers mysteries, witness of a such pompous
And pure indecency.
What? Because they do not dance as one dances
In the clubs; they urge me to call those splashes10
Office of church. Whence we
Do not see making wishes either piligrimages
For obtaining a holiness and a release11
Of having a bonny
Spirit the balmiest, the soul the most grateful,
To be the most equitable and less harmful,

IX

To be healed from the vanity, to be healed from
Need out of order of activity so dumb
And from bad raillery.
What idea the most bizarre than to imagine
A croward of religious who assemble or who glean
At certain days in a free
Room for welcoming a comedian who exists
Only for the pleasure that he gives or insists
To them, who in advance
Is payed yet. Therefore, it seems that I have to
Close theaters, or to pronounce severely too
On the very intense
State os comedian. Comedians remain

Dreamers who try to build a kingdom of God quite sane.
Sublime means happy in the improper sense. 2-revenues mesns
wealths, capitals, means. 3-distend means exaggerate. 4-slant
means success in the improper sense. 5-maul means abuse.
6-that he neglects, that being a relative pronoun od difference
is the complement of direct object of verb neglects. 7-and
that he cultivates, that being a relative pronoun of difference
is the complement of direct object of verb cultivates. 8- they
are devout, they replaces women. 9-rare means wonderful.
19-splashes means spectacles. 11- release means salvation.

Mistake and correction

I

The value of the reputation does not lie
In the manner in which it is expressed. In fact,
If it is thus used, it will inevitably
Be expressed in whatever way is most intact
And helpful to the receiver. This normally
Means that a change must be expressed in an exact
Language that, to attain its full efficacity,
The recipient can understand without shy1.

II

This does not necessarily means that this is
The highest level of the communication
Of which we are capable. It does not mean that
It is the highest levelof information
Of which you are capable. Now the whole aim at
The change is to raise level of communication,
Not to lower it by increasing the format3
Of fear; whence we have to get strong utterances.

III

For the misperception arises in turn from
The belief that the harm can be limited to
The body. That is because of underlying

Fear that the mind can hurt itself. None of thesefew
Mistakes is meaningful or decisive, seeing
That the miscreations of the mind do not too
Exist. This recognition is far better shielding
Device than any from of level stir4 at random,

IV

Because it presents correction at the level
Of error. It is essential to remember
That only mind can spawn5, that6 correction in kind
Belongs to the thoughtlevel. The body never
Exists except as a learning device for mind.
This learning is not subject to error
Of itsown, because it cannot create, find
Anything to produce because it is immobile.

V

Magic is the mindless or the miscreative
Use of mind. If you are afraid to use the mind
To improve, you should not attempt to do so.
The fact that you are afraid makes your mind declined
And vulnerable to miscreation. Hello!
A person who creates something wonderful, shined7
Is the expression of a right- mindedness in flow8,
If we want to say a mindedness so active.

VI

What selfish eye sees is not corrective, nor can
Mistake be corrected by any device that
Can be seen materially. As long as you greatly
Think in what your material sight does chitchat
You, your attempts at the correction will be
Misdirected. Real vision is obscure and mat9,

Because you cannot endure to see exactly
Your own inner defiled, shrined while you are human.

VII

So changeis an ability that grew after
Reparation, before which it was necessary.
The self-esteem rests on the comparison, and then
Compassion is a way of perceiving truly
Perfection or value of another even
If you cannot perceiveit in yourself. Really,
Compassion is a weaker reflection, often
A more powerful love-encompassment ever;

VIII

A more powerful love-encompassment that is
Far beyond any form of compassion you can
Conceive. Compassion is very essential to
Right-mindedness in the bound sense in which it then
Cannot be attained. For compassion is a true
Way of looking at another as if again
He had already gone far beyond his few
Actual accomplishments in time, he seizes10.
What has no real effect has no real existence.
Its effect is emptiness. I do not foster
Level confusion, but you must choose to correct
It. You would excute the insane behavior
On your part by saying you cannot, in effect,
Help it. Why should you condone thinking insaner?
There is a confusion here that you would do perfect11
To look at clearly like in a glass-appearance12.

XI

You may believe that you are responsible for
What you do, but not for what you think. Verity
Is that you are responsible for what you think,
Because it is at this level that you only
Show the choice. What you do comes from what you bethink
Or think. You cannot separate yourself truly
From truth in giving autonomy to the rank12
Behavior, behavior quite fair encore.

1-shy means fear. 2-information means communication. 3-format means aspect. 4-stir means confusion. 5-spawn means create. 6-that correction in kind, that a conjunctive pronoun is the complement of direct object of verb remember. 7-shined is a qualificative adjective of something. 8-flow means vogue. 9-mat means dull. 10-seizes means understand. 11-perfect means better. 12-glass-appearance means glassy surface, looking glass. 13-rank means fructuous, productive.

No 13

Forgiveness

I

Why must we then forgive? We forgive not only
Because otherwise
The life would not be viable. We normally
Forgive, for a wise,
For stopping the climbing of conflicts. We forgive
Before all because
We are all human beings and we can espouse, give
Our hands to good cause,
To the good habits, always commiserative.

II

We forgive because we understand that the joy
Of others depends
On us, and only the forgiveness can deploy
Or give life or hands
Back to human creatures. It exists certain cases
So sure of injustice
Where forgiveness seems to go against our duties,
Our rights not amiss
And the strictest. Pardon puts us in good places.

III

To forgive him, to him never! All, but not that!
This is him who had
Offended me, who destroyed my reputation at,
Who ruined me so bad.
This is not to me to do the first steps! Many
Often consider
The forgivenessas a cowardice, a vacancyl
Of the honor,
A capitulation in their rights as liberty!

IV

The forgiveness is simple only for the one
Who did not get to
Forgive. How many pardons miscarried in our own
Hearts, choked in our throats, too
Never blossomed out in our lips! How many lives
Get spoiled by an only
Pardon voluntarily refused, that arrives!
The refuse of truly
Pardoning can spoil all an existence, just dives.

V

It is not rare, at the occasion of a will,
To see brothers and
Sisters having it in for each other until
The death, that's in trend2.
If you may forget twigs or baubles, do not worry;
Even it is not
Easy; the experience proves it. How truly
May we forgive a lot
A rival who thrives over you in presidency?

VI

It is possible to reconcile totally
With him or her who
Betrayed our confidence, who spoiled our life, really
Who put a so few
Strain on the furture of innocent children? Then
On the plan strictly
Social, this is not easy, but it goes often
Otherwise on idea
Of the human quality because forgiveness
Is founded on free
Love. A hurt that is covered in business, in stress
Heals very slowly,
But we need mch time to take back your assuredness.

VII

For we cannot forget that the antiphaties,
The hates have the roots
Quite mysterious. Certain person thinks with ease
That one really doubts
To forgive because one cannot forget the wrongs
That other people
Caused to oneself. We cannot, as do certain thongs,
Normally mingle
The forgetfulness and forgiveness, no diphthongs.

VIII

The forgetfulness escapes at our will. This is
To forgive that men
Ask us. When, despite us, the thought of damages
Then proved comes back then
To our mind, far of discouraging us, we thus
Must benefit it

For renewing our forgiveness ads a surplus.
Whence it is a lit
Thing to know ads every person quite conscientious.

IX

To forgive, this is not forgetting. Forgiving,
This is encore more
Than forgetting. Forgiving, this is going
Above talent, therefore
This is giving over. Forgiving, this is changing
The heart of offended
And offender. Forgiving, this is a renewing3,
A restart ahead,
A mutation in our feelings, in our attitudes,
A love quite flowered
Again. Forgiving goes over order of rectitudes:
"What I sequestered
From you, I give it back to you, nothing more."
Yes, this is not that.
Forgiving belongs to the order of heart before
Whose the traits and pat
Characteristic is to beendless encore.
1-vacancy means lack in the improper sense. 2-in trend means in
vogue. 3-renewing means rebirth. 4-sequesterd means took.

No 14

United States

I

United-States reside _____ in the great continent
Of America, lure _____ in chastity, dreamy
Aspect, but full of pride, ___full of enlightenment,
Full of dignity, pure_____ as a ray that I see
To morning appearing.____ Ah! How I am joyous
Of being able to _____ look at me in your eyes!
And you are inspiring_____ me an innumerous
Esteem quite very due; ____ you are my tender sighs.

II

Your civility is _____ the triumph of talent,
Extention of system, _____ sharpened understanding,
Adaptive faculties, _____delight in arrangement,
Delight in stratagem, _____and delight in showing,
In comprehensible _____ results; this is a pretense
I long for keeping you_____ company. It is real
That you feel credible _____ honor that I advance
To the beauty so due _____of your marvels quite leal1

III

I descend to my turn_____ until you. I incline
Myself in front of you. _____ is not this you they name
America? I learn _____it by heart. Oh! your fine

Name, as you see too! _____i keep it as my frame.
You do not know ! you are ___ my winner. I could not
Resist to the power_____of your charms, then I am
Under force to disbar _____my thoughts without spot.
You are the nice flower _____that expands on my tram.

IV

And I put to your feet _____the honor of my faith.
Crazy I am not to_____have quite known to prepare
In your soul the concrete____fire-place where this rathe
Flame comes on, flame of true -------love then ready to wear
You out ; and that your heart_____ almost cannotlock up.
Open yourself to joy! _____Open yourself to mirth
That the heaven does part _____ to you in a nice cup!
I approach and employ _____ all my skills at your worth.

V

O America! You _____ feel that I have a clear
Head? This is not self-pride_____of my part, I wear you,
Each one then knows his true_____weight3 and his limit. Here
I would like that the guide _____ or understanding my few
Writings! You come to muse_____me some incomparable
Verses as ice to sun_____ I feel like melting my
Soul. Heats of hell quite ruse_____ do not equal my able
Heat. This is not a fun;_____for you, it is so high.

VI

O America you _____ agree that my sigh is
Quite tender and gracious!_____Writing would seem to be
To eyes what dance is to _____ to the limbs or to bodies.
In your bottom, I thus _____find theright property
Of writing: that is more _____than to fill me with joy.
Your nice aspects teach me _____the splendor of colors

And possession of lore3_____ forms; you make deploy
Ahead me so many _____ pictures, higher thinkers.

VIII

You offer me and I see _____so many higher thinkers
In the art. I perceive_____the poundless opulence
       Of pens, immunity4 _____
         in which several writers
Stand free and active_____ to choose out of immense
   Possible forms. The fair _____and different cultures
   In you add excitements _____ in invoking the aid
   Of other passions there _____by the poets. Features
In you are components _____ that make verses unfade
     1-leal means true. 2-weight means capacit. 3- lore
       is a qualificative adjective of forms and means
       knowledgeable. 4-immunity means indifference

No 15

Fraternal love

I

Love those who caused you annoyances.
Love them without wanting from them other
Thing than this: that they become better cronies.
If any friend, after being wrong, may encounter
Your look, ask your pardon,
And have you forgiven
If he does not ask pardon,
Ask him, you, if he then
Wants to be forgiven! If he does not demand
Forgiveness, ask him,you, if he thus wants to be
Pardoned! Love him several times he comes to you and
Approaches you, love him than before truly.

II

Who haveto do the first steps? Is not this offender?
Here this is not a matter of heart. There is no
Rule. But it regularly happens whatever
The offended who takes the initiative quite pro1
For this is the offender
Who lacked fraternity
Or charity who better
Needs to receive this free
Fraternity or charity. The great wounded
Is not the one that one dresses. The wide-open

Wounded, this is more offender than offended.
This is the offender who is the most fallen.

III

This is the offender who needs to be mended
And to be loved, the love fails in him. To forgive,
This is proving by the facts that the devoted
Is tied again. The collapsed brigges are during
Repaired. Let us keep this:
Since forgive means feel well,
Reconcile oneself, and this
Is not only to tell
Or say: "I do not forgive you, but I have nothing
To see with you." Forgiving, this is open
Your heart to other, not to close it. The pleasing
Perfection of love, this is the forgiveness, then.

IV

Another motive that may help us to forgive,
This is to recognize that the unfair talks or
The disagreeable attitudes of our active
Foes mean nothing. And then,
In our worst enemies,
We can discover often
The good sides. The worries,
The angers, the misunderstandings are often
The atternuating causes. For apostle
Paul told himself: "I do jnot do the good that I then
Want, and I do the evilthat I do not settle2.

V

How many unfortunate words uttered by us
In a time of impatience we would like to be
Able to catch up to, alas! As long as we thus
Count how many times we have pardoned our crony3,
We are not merciful,
We have not forgiven
Truly; this is the full
True sign of the pardon,
Of the nature that we are aware assings.
This is to always forgive! The man may have rights
On another man. But theserights are littlke things
In comparison with what he owes back for sights
Of the welldoingsof nature as the blessings.

VI

The nature gave us infinitely more than
That we could never lend to other man: the life,
Our body with its senses and its faculties, then
The frredom, the sea, the trees, the flowers, the rife
Birds. At las, then the man
Is a wolf for man! Hardly
Forgiven for a debt,
Our man to whom one then
Left this debt for him yet
Comes back against a poor who owed him one hundred
Dollars and treats the poor with the last cruelty
By putting him in jail. No matter how much ahead
The wretched man throws himself at his feet sadly,
Begs him, asks a delay.
The other, forgetting
Rapidly every day
His former corresponding

Situation, closes pitilessly his heart
And surrenders him at the justice. Look at
How the human beings treat each other. The smart
Law of menin comparison with man is hot
And inflexible hardness,
Unless the therapy
Conscience of the address
Of speeches normally
Comes to tame the wolf that is in the man!
This is not a virtue to take birth from a noble
Blood, but to raise as I do it, this is again
The high virtue and the nobles quite veritable.
1-pro means supportive. 2-settle means want in the improper
sense. 3-crony is written at the singular because of the rhyme

No 16

Misinterpretation

I

Since I am the servant
Of the men, I am firm encore
To put me to advancement
Of all, and to use me for
All of you the friends of nicer
Words quite so perfume. Feeling
So normal of my tender
Heart are enough of making
Me fraternal for all creatures
Why is the fraternal love
The sign by the fine features
By which men can know above
Everything each other? Because
The fraternal love until
The unity, without cause, is humanly unreal1.

II

The man surrenders to law
Of this selfish world cannot
Quickly renounce to his raw2
Interest, to his pride as lot,
To his susceptibility,
To his will of domination,
To his lies and jealousy,

To his devaluation.
When this fraternal love too
Exists even imperfectly,
When the human beings few3
Enjoy it together truly,
Then this love becomes the sign
Of the irruption of joy
On the earth! Loving a fine
Human being, not as toy,

III

This ia addressing him the call
The strongest and most needed,
This is waking up and all
Moving in him a shrouded
And mute being, who cannot
Stop oneself appearing to
Our voice, a being so hot4
That even the one who
Carrie it did not know it
Although he sees it for first
Time, is very explicit;
A being who is loved, versed
Truly does not recognize
Itself. For helping us forgive
Promptly to our allies5,
To our colleague quite active.

IV

It is not enoughto then
Recognize our parts of great
Responsibility in
The antipathies or hate

Or anger that exist in us
And our fellows? So many
Divorces, quarrels, surplus5,
Sullen persons, vanished very
Soon in certain families
If only we wanted to
Stop us a while with ease
For judging with a true
And more impartial spirit
And a heart more merciful
That parts us from our concrete
Fellows, that we are pitiful.

V

There many persons who
Live in the same house, belonging
Sometimes at the same true
Family, linked for living
Together in the joiner7
Of charity, and natheless
Do not speak to each other
Since several years. The cause is this:
They find it quite often
In a profound selfishness,
A conceit without certain
Indulgence, a defenselessness8
Quite skittish, a tenacious
Obstinacy, a pretense
On his proper conduct, thus
A discord or difference.

VI

Wit a little humility
A good will, it would be so
Easy to understand really
Each other and apropos
To do the part of things. For
Judging very exactly
An imputed fault encore
To the fellows where we
Call ourselvesthe victims, for
Caring for the rapports quite
Hurt and attributed more
To the vice of other, right
Now would not we have to set
Ourselves on one of platfoms
Of scale? All the faults have root
The most cruel on all forms.

VII

When we complain about flaw9
It happens to us to make
Sufficiantpart of our raw10
Impressionality, sake11,
Of our emotivity,
And of our weak spot12 and stand13.
There are some14 who normally
Increase truth, who understand,
Interpret certain awry
Words or certain acts always
Indifferent without wee
Consequence! A word or phrase
Quite fallen in conversation
Or slipped from the pen, without

Unmoral aspiration,
Is taken in wrong part by doubt
Or by a suspicious spirit:
From a grain of sand it makes
A hill, from a mouth a lit
Elephant! There are all sakes15.

VII

A joke quite told for gheering
Up becomes a disaster
In the mind of this crooking
Person who does enregister
Everything, who does remark
Everything, and who unites
The fact, this word being not dark
To the anterior sights
Or observations and in fact
A stuff that his natural
Imagination so intact
Alternates so dismal
Colors like a pleasure! For
Those people strive hard to rack
My brain and to torture more
The others who are so slack17!

1-unreal means irrealisable, unpratical. 2-raw means natural. 3-few is anadverb and means a little. 4-hot mean new in the improper sense. 5- allies means fellows. 6-surplus means excess. 7-joiner means link. 8defenselessness means susceptibility. 9- flaw means fault. 10-raw means natural. 11 sake means motive. 12-spot means susceptibility. 13-stand means way of seeing thing. 14 some = some persons. 15-sakes means motive. 16-sights written at the plural because of the rhyme. 17-slack means slow-moving, slow-paced.

No 17

Rebirth

I

The pessimists are always persuaded to
Have the good reasons of distorbing of their suite1
Who deceives them. On the contrary, they are true
Or sure, if it is the state,
That this was required! And in
Supposing that this was straight2
Required, have not again
Provoked? If we persuade that our fellows have
Not been for us what we estimate that they would
Have to be, why not to ask us if we then crave,
Will remain for them all what we had to and could.

II

The discords or misunderstandings are springing
Up again in step to our incapacity
To understand others. The msan is ignoring
The femininepsychology, and the lady,
This one of man! How many
Hurts we could spare to each other
Reciprocally if we
Could understand each other
Mutually!to practice the merciful or
To give faults, for me, this is nevertheless
To revalorize us, this is to rebuild more

In us all what wickednesshad destroyed, not less;

III

This is a veritable rebirth! Our proper
Enemi the most to be afraid, the nearest,
The most frightening, this is our fellow-helper,
This flesh is subject to the wrongs that truly pressed
Us or brought us to the vice,
This flesh that is against
The righteousness and who twice
Opposes in us the minced
Penchants of nature with the impressions of joy.
Enemi is all the funiest that we carry
Endlessly with us, as a child with his nice toy,
That it is not other thing thamn ourselves only.
Oit is not one of our senses,
Not one of our faculties
That does not tempt us with ease
And that thus does not release.
The passions ferment more or less in all the hearts
And in all the minds: this is the pride that take us
Away, this is the greed that set us a trap as parts
Of life, this is the envy that torments us thus;

IV

This is the impurity that would want to stain
In us the body and the soul, this is the anger
That piques3 us, this is the gluttony that does gain4
Us, these are laziness and idleness that ever
Teach us all the vices. For
This hardship of flesh is then
Extremely painful encore
For those who like to remain

Good. This flesh is an enemi whose we cannot
Get rid of it, whatever we do, we can lessen
It, wee can subdue it, but it is always thereat,
Alive and exigent and murmuring often,

V

When you do not please it; it descends into
All the excesses when we loosen the bridle.
Do you know the means for resisting to
The bad temptations? We must be natural
Or sincere with ourselves and
We must think that vanity
Always exists. Before
Enumerating the way
So positive for encore
Defeating the temptations, we point out that it
Is quite elementary of fleeing at first
The occasion! We are friends together, th lit
Experience ot the past must favor the versed
Prudence. It is unitile
Tpo put the straw into fire
And to pray only a futile
Divinity quite higher
So that it does not burns. If voluntarily
You put yourself in a next occasion of great
Wickedness and that you do nothing for really
Getting out of it, do not surprise to have new bait6.
1-suite means followers in the improper sense. 2-straight is
an adverb. 3- the dots of suspension replace to be. 4-piques
means irritates. 5-gain means obtain, solicit. 7-therat
means at that place. 8- bait means temptations.

No 18

Temptation

I

We do not have to play with temptation:
Yielding a little, this is weakeing
Ourselves and not to weaken flirtatrion1,
The first concession is the source of the falling
Over. The idleness is
The mother all the vices.
The habitual miseries
Give rise to the malices
Or to the temptations. Then, be joyful, always
In good humor. When we will be tired to work, let
Us sing! And the bad idea will dance! All the days,
The habit of empire on ourselves helps us yet
So much to take away again
Temptations. This will be thus,
For example, the chagrin
Of sensesthat the specious
Of soul. The one who cannot watch his eyes cannot
Watch his heart. The regard produces the thought that
Can provoke the desire, the consentment, the flat
Habit, the necessity, and the death. A lot,
That helps us to understand
The reflection of a man
Being blind. The countermand
And the vigilance often

Makes us avoid the temptations without delay,
As soon as it appears. Let us suffocate it
From its birth, otherwise, if we let it grow one day,
We will not come any longer of it
For the temptations seems often
A spark thatcan consume all
A forest but that we can
Snuff it out by putting all
Both feet on it without hurt. What an imprudence
If, being able to snuff it out the start,
We let it snuff out itself so much that we thence
Can become its masters! Let us talk as a smart
Man that the temptation is
With the human condition.
The bad men search commentaries
To divert from their position
Other men. Do not permit that we are really
Convinced by the temptations of the evil. Whence
Do not let us submit to the bewitchery2
Of discouragement, egoism and vengeance,
Hanger, indifference,
Domination, amplitude.
Again today, the intense
Modern men, dazzled3 by good
Power of their technical ingineerings, by
The variety of their great inventions, and
By distance to which their colloquies can reach, their high
Influences and their glances; those men have some grand
Conscience to increase their proper values and to
Measure their statures from their realization true.
Flirtation means temptqation. 2-bewitchery means temptation.
3-dazzled by good, dazzled being an adjectivepast participle of men

No 19

Forgiveness and forgetfulness

I

What is particularly
Remarkable, this is its extreme
Facility. Sometimes when we
Exhort those who normally seem
To undergo the harms to fair
Reconciliation. There are
Certain men who tell with an air
So tight-lipped and very bizarre:

II

"Forgive, but I do not forget.
This is to say that they do not
Forgive, in the bottomof wet
Heart, those persons maintain a lot
A secrete melancholy,
A tenaciousanger that1, at first
Occasion, blow up and produce truly
Make again a quarrel so worst!

III

Such a meanessis in the heart
Of each of us. Our forgiveness
should be universal: as part

Of life without exception, less
We should be easy: with bounty
And indulgence, we should be then
Merciful: by forgetting truly
All hurts, after having forgiven.

IV

The first step, this is to love
Our enemies. It is enough
To forgive with point of lips, above
It is necessary that tough
Heart goes to the victim. We should
Not wait, more we wait, more the true
Reconciliation becomes rude
And difficult. Do the first steps with good......2

V

Here, we have to understand
From what love it is matter.
Be careful not to make comprehend
This love of our enemis proper3
In a natural appeal, in
An affectionate well-wishing
For them. By prescribing us then
To love them, men ask nothing........4

VI

The second step, this is to render
To our enemies the good for
Evil. Occasions to do better
Will never fail when we therefore
Will want to look for them. It is
Not always possible to render

To our enemies the services
Quite material, bread-and-butter;

VII

But it is possible and even
Easy to speak to them that they
Are in good terms, to set off then
Their qualities. This is today
A welldoing that has its value
And when those good words reach the ears
Of an enemi; they move too
Him, more agreeable than favors5

VIII

If we want to forgive promptly
Our fellows, is not it enough
Sometimes to remind the very
Numerous pardonsquite so tough
That we received from another?
At first, if we repassed, from year
To year, from weak to weak together
With our lives, quite so unsincere;

IX

If we remind in the quarter
That we lived, to the relations
That we maintained, to the greater
Jobs and in our nice vocations
That we practiced, surely that we
Overthrow the unnemerous
Faults that so many persons truly
Have entirely forgiven us.

1-a tenacious anger that, that being a relative pronoun of melancholy and anger is the subject of blow up and and produce and make. The dot of suspension replaces will. 3-proper being a qualificative adjectiveofenemies est placed after the common noun Because of rhyme. 4- the dot of suspension replaces similar.

No 20

Pity

I

Let us think of faults so intence
That we havecommited during
The chilwood, the adolescence,
The youth, the rapist or full-growing
Age! For lack of nature, against
The others, aginst ourselves.,
The others, against ourselves, and
Against common welfair! I minced1
The words for the sake of the grand.......2

II

If another person has been
Merciful toward us, how can
We be hard, exigent and keen3
Against our fellows? And again,
Do you have rights to act this way?
Are we dead for saving our men,
We who are so mean at their stray4?
For pity'sake, a little sweetness then!

III

Ah! It is so natural to
Detect and to hate those who then
Just hurt us! It is easy too
To fight them by remetting often
The evil for the evil, and
Even a little more! This is
Easy for us to understand
Our rights in fighting our cronies.

IV

It is easy for us to gess
In our rights for fighting those who
Cause us the unhappiness
Without consideration, too
By all the means, those blind poor men,
Without asking if them also,
As us, they do not have even
The soul to rescue apropos.

V

From our time, many people think
That killing a person, this is
Against the best method to cranck6
to learn them to live and to please!
Instead of detesting them, and
If we try to build the seat
Of thosehearts and to tempt by a grand,
True love to coquer them with wit7.

VI

Fror helping us to forgive promptly
Our fellows, would not it suffice
One more time to normally
Recognize our part of sacrifice
Or responsibility in
The antipathies or angers
That exist between us and them8, then?
So many divorces and ruptures
Soon would disappear in certain
Households, if only we wanted
To stop for judging with an even9
Mind and with a heart more sainted10.

1-mincedmeans moderated. 2-the dots of suspension replace politeness. 3-keen means malicious. 4-stray meansimmigrant worker. 5-guess means believe in the improper sense. 6-crank means start in the improper sense. 7- wit means humor. 8- them replaced fellows. 9-even means impartial. 10- sainted means compassionate, full of mercy.

No 21

Mercifulness

I

Here, you would not haveto believe
That I oppose myself to great
Growth of the science so active,
Far to be there. This is not straight
Science that is in cause, further
The pretenseof the man to set
Itself up as absolute master
Of his destiny and also yet.

II

For the modern man, to be present
In this world, this is to judge it,
To manipulate it, to repent
It, to exploit it, to profit
From it. Or if there is a thought
That is uniquely strange to me,
This is that one to guide, as naught,
Men and to have on them a grit.

III

The weight of love that I should lay
On my life win on the weight of hate
That then weighs on the other tray

Of balance. I have to go straight
To the goal and attack the sin1
By its root for stopping bothering.
The evil sticks upon the skin
Of man all long of his being2.

IV

It3 is thus everywhere present.
The good itself is null and void
From evil as kernel fragment
Is mixed to good grain quite devoid.
We dan expect that evil can
Move back and lessen itself in
The measure where the love often
Grows and attains a stage quite even.

 V

"Spare us from the evil" thus means:
Spare us from that part that is out
Of love in ourselkves as our scenes.
For physical harms that can put
Us or afflict us, the ones then
Escape at our power, we remain
Powerless to prevent them, even
To avoid them, not to obtain.......3

VI

Such those blows and those spasms that
Promptly spread the devastation
And ruin in the cities quite prat,
In the campains, in the nation.
Those are: the cyclones, the earquakes,
The floods, microbes, avalaches,

Tidal waves create headaches,
Pests, contagious diseases;

VII

The insects that destroyed our harvest.
It existsanother species
Of the physical injuries
Whose we are the authors. At least,
It only depends on us to
Suppress them. Those injuries
Result from violation of true4
Laws by an abuse of privileges:

VIII

There are so many diseases:
Ailments, born disorders, retarded,
Syndromes, thus introduce with ease
In our organs via by ill-bred
Excess in the usage of things
Put by our disposition, by
Disobedience to law-writtings
Of nature, posed by wisdom of its high.......5

IX

The libertinage marks the flesh
Of a deep stimag. That does not
Mean that all sick patients are fresh
And guilty, far from there. A lot,
For those bad loucks whose we are
Artisans, that is enough, for
Being rescued from them so far,
To practice the virtue encore.

X

Our eye-glasses are distorting.
We the same things and we do
Not see the alikeness during.
This is for that I insist too
In order that we transform
The way we see the things, and then
I invite you to guard, to form
Us against judgment that we strengthen6.

XI

For seeing quite well, we have to
Start by purifying our inner
Looks, that means the heart. Someone who
Is good, ready at all whatever
People with good feelings and good
Intentions. When we love someone,
We are ready to forgive. We could
Say that love blinds us, makes us one.

X

If unfortunately, we do
Not love someone, the least trifle
Takes proportions quite so undue
And unfair. It is possible
After in such conversations
Or body languages where human
Beings only see confabulations
thus bad and quite so inhuman,

XI

We have to also discover
The aspirations of good deed
Although we think of it, no
One is eotally bad, wicked?
Thus not to do wrong, this is better.
But not to do good, this is worst.
What do good works and prayer
Serve that end to think to be first.......7

XII

The money is one of vital
Evils and causes much misfortune.
It hardens the heart of total,
Renders him slave and opportune
And envious, makes him practice8
Murders and evoke wars, does create
Injustices, removes the peace
And bliss, makes him immoderate.

1-sin means evils, wrongs. 2-beings means life in the improper sense. 3-it is everywhere, it replaces sin. 4-the dots of suspension replace them. 5- true means natural. 6-the dots of suspension replace author. 7-strengthen means bring. The dots of suspension means perfect. 0-practice means commit in the improper sense.

No 22

Peace

I

The peace is not the selfish possession
Of the life,
Protected1 from others, but an expression
Of a rife2
World to build with others, in the harmony.
I invite
You to be a tool of peace, I only
Put in sight
That peace needs from our parts a challenging
Effort. Then
You agree with me that establishing
The peace in
The world is not an easy work! This is
The immense
Work of all a life. A world of the ease
Or peace, whence
This is doubtlessly a world where the war
Then does not
Exist. This is much more than that encore3.
That's a fat4
Where the human beings live together5,
Thus accept
Each other and naturally savor,
Interpret,

Love each other in a completory6
Service, at
Every level of the humanity
Thereat.

II

Consequently, this is a world where hate,
The envy,
The war are regretted, avoided straight7,
Peace truly
Is a gift, also reconciliation
Between man
To man. The man in cooperation8
With the man
Finds back peace with himself. A criminal
Is really
A man insidely broken, in critical
Quandary,
Devoured, totally dismembered, exploided
By thefear
And the shame to those who are needed
How to spear9
The peace in their daily lives. To dare making
The peace, not
A peace that is shy; not an offering
For a spot
Of peace offering of all rest, for having
The calmness;
Not a peace quite condescending, yielding,
And unless
A peace of the love, a peace quite tenacious,
Stubborn and
Combative that can engender thus
Love and fan.

III

The peace has nothing muffled, insensible.
Furthermore,
It has a voice, of bowels that wiggle10,
That encore
Open up to all the human problem,
With a heart
Quite reconciled. Do not let the items
Make us part11.
We leave more to understand and to feel,
To love for
Carrying the attitudes of the real
Peace more
In the suffering world where we leave thus.
For let you
Approach, let you put aside enormous
Bars that do
Separate the onesfrom others. Today,
Be the voice
Of speechless people. Do in such a way
That all choice12
Men may tender their hands to each other,
Together
Rejoin. When the reign of love will proffer
Or offer
To all the human beings of the whole
World without
Any exclusion of race, of role,
Religion, doubt.

IV

This is to say that13 we love to such
A degree
All the human beings that14 we made much
Normally
Disappear in our life at first, in the life
Of other;
Next in the laws, the rapports15 of the rife
Great power
And of oppression of the rich on poor,
Of the man
On woman, of the white on black, encore
Of strong then
On weak, that16 we relate henceforth are
Normally
Based on the justice, on the so bizarre
Equality,
On the mutual love. Let us realize thus
What human
Beings expect at each moment from us,
We who then
Are ladies and sons, brothers and sisters
Between us.
In order that children become brothers,
We have thus
To nourish them and to cherish them. For
All love, even
The most striving, knows clouds and coolings, more
Sometimes then
The ruptures. But sincethe love is very
Necessary17
To man for keeping on living, really
It must be
When it is hurt and broken. The patent

Medicine
To broken love is precisely the permanent
And serene
Forgiveness. To be forgiven and
Forgiving,
To be loved until the pardon and
Thus loving
Until forgiveness: such is object of
This requirement.
But the one who enjoys the life with love
Will live content.

1-protected from others, protected being an adjective past participleof possession. 2- rife means universal. 3-encore is an adverb and means again. 4- fat means the best or richest part, a necessary part; fat replaces world in the allegorical sense. 5-together means in harmony. 6-completory nmeans reciprocal. 7-straight is an adverb. 8-cooperation means peace in the improper sense. 9-spear means lance, put, shoot. 10-wiggle means shake, tremble. 11- part means divide. 12 choice is a quailificative adjective of men and means extraordinary. 13-this is to say that, that being a conjunctive pronoun is the complement of direct object of verb say. 14- all the human beings that we made make, that being a relative pronoun of human beings is the complement of direct object of verb make. 15-rapports is the subject of verb are. 16-and that we relate, trhat being a relative pronoun of rapports is the complement of direct object of verb relate. 17-necessary means indispensable.

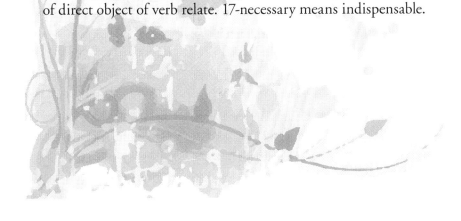

No 23

Useless war

I

Among all leaders who preside empires of world,
Cerulean is one of the first rank, and there is
The department of Central West. He descended
One day in the house of agent B, on the pearled
Road of middle town, and told him: "agent B, follies
And excess of Teleman who pretented
To be the powerful
Countryin Central West
Attracted my brimful
Anger:I held as best
Yesterday a meeting at United Nations
For knowing if Otan may be able to crack
Down or scold1. Teleman, or it2 may be able
To destroy it. Go in all its immense stations3,
Then examine everything; and you will come back
To give me a description quite reliable4.
And I will decide on
Your report to correct
It5 or will fire upon
It6." Lord, at your respect,
Told agent B: "I have never been in this land;
I know nobody in it7.__ So much the better,
You will not be partial; you received from heaven
The discernment, and I augment to it the grand

Gift of inspiring you the confidence; saunter8,
Observe, do not fear, you will welcome again."

II

Agent B took an air plane and left with his agents.
At the end of some stays, he met through the flatlands
Of Danton the telemian armies that
Want to take over the worldwide trade that augments,
He presented himself to a soldier who stands
Up away from. He talked to him and asked him what
Was the motive of war.
The chief answered: "I know
Nothing; this is not encore
My business; apropos9,
My job is to kill and to be killed for earning
My own life; who I serve, that means nothing for me.
In the future, I cpould pass in the opponent
Camp; whence somebody told me: "Other is giving
Much money to their whole soldiers more than we
Do not have in this cursed service. If you enchant
To know why one fight each
Other, talk to my fair
Captain." For the unrich
Soldier is unfair.
Agent B having made a bare gift to soldier,
Got into the camp. He soon made the acquaintance
With the Captain, and asked him the motive of war.
Captain replied: "What do you from me earlier
To know? I live five miles frm here; I heard the dense
War is powerful declared against us more.

III

"Whence I left immediately my family;
And I am going to look for, according to
Our custom: the fortune or the death; attended
That I have nothing to do." Agent B nicely told :
"Your comrades are not little instructed and due
Than you." Captain replied: "Thereare only our head
Principal satraps who
Know so precisely why
One kills each other." Too
Surprised and very shy,
Agent B introduced himselfto generals;
He came in their familiarity. And then
One of them told him at last the cause of this war
That destroys since ten yeatrs the individuals
Of Central West, came from all a quarrel often
Between werstern and Eastern for the furthermore
Trade. Vice-president of great
Cerulean and ours
Worthily support straight
Rights of their governors.
Dispute got warmes. One put everywhere an army
Of a million of soldiers. This army must
Be recruites all ten years at a big value
Of five hundred thousand men and women.really,
The murders, fires, ruins, devastatiuons quite unjust
Are added; universe suffes; wraths continue.

IV

Our prime minister and the one of eastern keep
Often protesting, they onlyact for welfare
Of their own countries; and at each protestation,
There are always some cities destroyed11 and some deep

Provinces ravaged12. Next day, a rumor quite fair
Came to circulate that this hard altercation
Must be ended; for
General of Eastern land
And ours hasten to more
Fight, it was cruel and
Bloody. Agent Bsaw all faults and all species
Of abominations in it12, he was witness
Of wrong hands of principal satraps, then he saw
Officers killed by their own troops; in the cities,
He saw soldiers who achievesto kill breathless
Comrades who wereexpiring. He went in the raw
Hospitals where they brought
Wounded persons whose most
Of them expired by fraught
Neglect quite almost
Inhuman from those that the government just paid
Highly to help them. Agent Btold: Áre they men
Or ferocious animals? Ah! I see quite how
Teleman will be destroyed and very afraid.
Occupied by this thought, he passed in the golden
Camp of Eastern for knowing hidden details now.

V

He was more welcomed in the camp of Eastern land than
That one of Teleman, according to what
Has been predicted to him, he saw the same
Excesses that surprised him with horror. And then
He told himself: Oh! Oh! Oh! angel Samarat!
If you want to exterminate with a warred flamed
The telemanians,
it is so important
That Angels of Sanians
Burned eastern land. Content

To inform more in detail of what happened thus
In the one and the other army, he then
Learned from the great action of generosity.
From greatness of soul, from humankind so precious
That amazed him and ravished him. He often
Exclaimed: "Inexplicable people, how truly
Can you put together
So much blaseness and so
Much greatness, and further
So much virtue as show
And so much crime? Nevertheless, the peace were thence
Declared. Chiefs of both armies who, none has won
For their unique interests, had blood of so many
Men poured, their fellows, went to lobby their precious
Rewards in their courses. They honored peace upon
The written publics and both governments. Daily,
They announced that the return of continuous
Felicity and of permanent virtue on
The land where people come back to their duty.

1-scold means punish. 2-or if it may be, it replaces Otan. 3-stations
command posts. 4-reliable means sincere, faithful. 5-to correct
it, it replaces Teleman. 6- Will fire upon it, it replaces Teleman.
7-know no body in it, it replacesTeleman. 8-saunter means walkin
the improper sense. 0- apropos is a preposition. 10- destroyed isan
adjective past participle of cities. 11- ravaged is an adjective past
participle of provinces. 12- abomination in it, it replaces fight.
13-chiefs are the subject of verb went. 14-both armies who, who
being a relative pronoun of armies is the subject of verb had.

No 24

Story of Pan Mick

I

I heard about a religious doctrine that they1
Call "believe",
The celestial truth that came in an only day,
Spreads, make perceive
Itself through the earth. It2 will be necessary
That we will kill
Ourselves to study a solar eclipse truly
Lasting until
Three days in Greece3,after Cristo4 raised from the dark;
And they array5
In the almanac that asks us to yearly mark6
This godly day.

II

The indecisive father said: "My son was quite
Overjoyed. Thus,
What will the tutor then teach my son very bright7?
The capricious
Tutor answered: "To be friendly, and if he knows
The ways to cheer8,
He will know all; this is an art that one learn, shows
In the Zephyr
College of theology without offering9
The least of pain."

The mother hugged the nice and uncultivating
Tutor so vain.

III

And then she said: "I all see that you are the man
The most knowing
About the matters of the sky and of the earth. Pan11
Will be owing
You all his education. I guess that there will
Be nothing wrong
If Pan learns few stories."__ He answered:" you are real,
Wise in your long
Thought, but what this story used for? There is surely
The most utile
And the most agreeable than daily story
So inutile.

IV

All old stories, as one of our great thinkers told,
Are only the fixed10
And conventional tales officially controlled11;
And for the mixed
Moderns, this is a chaos that person cannot
Unravel." Then
The father exclaimed: "Mister the tutor, you spot
Minds of children
With a mass of inutile knowledge the most
Absurd and vain;
And this one that is the most able almost
To choke all sane
Kind of genius, this is the human language
That God used to
Speaking to his servants. Those divine and so mage12

Brought the taboo13
And endless conflicts very bloodthirsty between
The heirs of God.
There is another fact that chokes the serene
Talent14 Of cad15:

V

"This is revelation. The revelation is
Only a bad
Joke. My son does not have to dry out or to freeze
His brain in those mad
Studies. If a day he needs a nice surveyor
To draw the plan
Of sky and earth, he will make them, as a payer,
Survey again
For his money. Whence if he wants to separate
Antiquity
From its noble-men, that comes back up to private
Times, normally
He will go and look for a chaste Benedictine.
A gifted man
Is not either singer, or musician, or dean,
Or a craftsman,
Or lawyer, or doctor, but he can make all arts
Thrive16 by whetting17
Them by his magnificence; all arts are the parts
Of life18 being."

VI

The tutor says: "You have well noticed that the grand
End of the man
Is to succeed in the society quite planned19.
And this is then

In what they20 have very much great reason to tell
That gentlemen
Of quality (I agree those who are so21 well
Wealthy again)
Know everything without having apprised22 nothing,
Because they23 know
In long run to judge things that he is ordering,
That he pays so.

VII

Madam says: "The charms of my son start in the world,
He cannot turn
Off his genius by study of all those curled24
Trashes so stern25;
But at last what would my son learn?" Tutors answered:
"As I tell you,
He is a man who may sparkle, by his manners,
Thus in the few
Chance or in the occasion. The nature, that26 just
Makes everything,
Gave him a talent that28 will be spread and that29 must
Be spread with king30
And prodigious success, and this will be to sing
Agreeably
The celestial and earthly words of worshiping
God. The ritzy3i
Graces32 of the youth, joint33 with this superior
Gift, will make him
See as the young men who will have the most prior34
Hope with the vim35."

VIII

She believes to be the mother of a well-made
Mind and gives to
Intelligent persons of New York the well-paid36
Supper to view
Quite sparkling. The head of young man is reserved37, then
He just acquires
The art of talking without getting38 on again
And he inspires
Better in the custom of not being proper
To nothing. When
His father sees him eloquent, he weeps over
His fault so sudden
Not to have made him39 learn the Latin, he would buy
For him a long
Chasuble40 for him. Madam says: "No, we can try
To buy among
The garments some high-priced suits for him, for there is
In the suit more
Money than in the chasuble. She who pleases
To keep encore
The noble feelings, will deal to sollicitate
A regiment
For him, by expecting she will spend a lot straight41;
This resplendent
Family is exhausted more to live in style
Of lords. Often
To have an expensive wife, this is to exile
In a hard dent.

IX

A young widowed of dignity who truly is
Their neighbor, who
Has only a poor fortune, wants to put with ease
In strength42 the true
Value of their properties, and by espousing
Their young born-rich
Man. She43 attracts him through her, sees herself loving,
Makes him reach
And perceives that he is not so indifferent,
Drives him nicely,
Enchants him, captivates him. She gives sometimes meant44
Praise, sometimes wee
Advices; she becomes the best friend of father
And mother. Whence
An old friend proposes a proper and tender
Marriage. Thence
The parents45, amazed46 by flame47 of this alliance,
Accept with joy
The proposition: they give, without remonstrance,
Their unique boy48.

X

The young man goes espouse a woman that he
Adores so much
And whose he is loved; the friends of the house really
Compliment such
His decision. It is a morning to the knees
Of the charming
Spouse that the love, the esteem and the decencies,
Give him during
The course of his life; he tastes the first signs of their made
Happiness; whence

They plan to lead a delicious life, when the maid
Of madam thence
Arrives quite alarmed. And there are other private
News, she shatters:
The bailiffs moved the furniture out; all the great,
Rude creditors
Grapped everything. Let us go to see, the born rich
Says, what is it,
This adventure?__ The spouse tells: yes, go to reach
Them and to split......49

Xi

He runs and arrives at the house; his father
Was in jail yet.
All domestics escaped each of their side, further
He feels like wet,
By carrying all stuffs that they could. The madam
Is alone, tears
Helplessly; nothing left to her only the sham50
Thoughts51 and sham cheers52
Of her fortune, of her beauty, of her mistakes,
Of her crazy
Expenses, of her extravagances; she shake
Naturally.

XII

The born-rich man53, astounded54 to see this bitter
Shameful event,
The rage in the heart, goes to look for his former
Wise informat55,
Unloads the harm from his belly, and ask him some
Good advices.
This mature man proposes him, with much wisdom

Or with vices,
To make himself tutor of children. The aching
Heart says: "At first,
I do not know anything; you learned me nothing;
You are the worst
And the first cause of my misfortune." The tutor
Laments with trance46
And tells him: "try to be a better editor
In an immense
Company of review. This is an excellent
And so provided
Resource in America. The young gallant56,
More disappointed
Than ever, runs to find the pastor of his mother;
An accreditation
Of man who only guides the women of higher
Consideration;
As soon as he sees the rich man, he quickens through
Him 57 at his ease.
Eh! My God! Mister Pan, and where is your brand-new
Car ? and how is
Your respectable the madam your wealthy mother?
Poor man then tends
To count familial disasters to preacher
Who reprimands.

XIII

As much as he explains what was happened, pastor
Shows a rude look,
More indifferent, and really comes to aver58:
"My son, God took
Everything because God wants you; any fortune
Serves to corrupt
The heart; God in his mercy tends to opportune,

To interrupt
And to reduce your mother to begging. She will
Spend all her way
To serve God; much better she is sure of her real
Salvation." Eh!
My father, by expecting, would not have the done
Means to obtain
Some help in the world. The pastor says: "All are gone;
There is a sane
Servant who expects me in my office." This man
Is ready to
Faint; he is treated likely same by his laden49
Friends, he learns too
Better to know religion and world in a half
Day than all rest
Of his life. As he is plunged in the despair, no laugh,
In his arrest.
He sees coming a convertible car; truly,
He sees inside
A man quite unrefined, fleshy and fresh, who50 breathes
In all the side
The sweetness and the gaiety, who then unseethes51
His lump slender
Wife, enough rudely agreeable, is rolled next
To him. Driver
Stops and contemplates the rich man, in the contest,
Who looks phallic
In his dolor, wonder: Eh! My God! I believe
That this is Mick,
My friend, who disregarded me, I conceive
This is him. Then
The driver jumps and runs to hug his former friend.
Mick sees Aven:
The shame and tears cover his face. He feels like fiend.

XIV

Aven says: "You abandoned me; but you are great
Lord, I still love……..59"
Mick, troubled60 and sad, counts him, by creeping, his state
In a part of
Story. "come in the hotel where I lodge, to count
Me the rest, then
Aven tells: "Hug my wife, let us go with my gaunt61
Wife to waken62
And to dine at the same time. My wife and me feel
Glad to help you.
Do not be nobleman; all the grantors quite leal63
Of this world do
Not lift my friend. You come back with me; and I learn
You this job, then
It is not difficult; I put you in Eastern
We live again
Glad in the corner of land where we are truly
Born." Meanwhile Mick
Feels himself shared between pain and hilarity64;
The shame comes quick;
Tenderness comes slow, he wonders: "All my rich friends
Betrayed me, and
Aven that I despised, comes to my help as godsends.
What fair and bland
Instruction! Bounties of the soul of Aven form
In the whole heart
Of Mick the seed of good natural that the firm
World in its part
Would not have strangled. He feels that he could not live
Away from his
Mother and his father. Aven says: "We believe
That with our ease
We will take care of your mother; as for your good

Father being

In jail, I heard the affairs; his creditors65 could

See that nothing

Left for him, will agree for much buck; I will take

Care of that." Then

Aven puts the father out of prison. All make

Both friends often

Happy. Mick returned in his superb-native land

With his parents

Who take back their first profession quite very planned:

He compliments

His good friend and he espouses the young sister

Of Aven, whence

She66 earns the same good humor with he brother,

Has a good sense,

And makes him very happy. The father of Mick

And his mother

And Mck see now that the vanity kills so quick67

The real rapture.

1-that they call, they replaces people. 2-it will be necessary, it is an impersonal pronoun subject. 3-this is a story about a solar eclipse that lasted three days in Greece, after the sun appeared; the people said that Cristo the said that cristo died and raised after three days. 4-Cristo was the god of sun in the Greek culture..5-array means expose, place, arrange, put. 6-mark means remember, recall, honor, celebrate in the improper sense. 7- bright means splendid. 8-cheer means please. 9-offering means giving.10-fixed means arranged. 11- Controlled is an adjective past participle of tales. 12-mage means wise, magical. 13- taboo means sacred. 14-talent means genius.15-cad mens person. 16-thrivemeans encourage. 17-whetting means bloom, blossom. 18-life uses as a qualificative adjective of being and means human, active, alive, living. 19-plannedis a qualificative adjective of society.20- in what they, they replaces people. 21- So well is an adverb. 22- apprised means learned. 23-because they know, they replaces gentlemen.24- curled means twisted and turned. 25- stern means difficult. 28-that just makes everything, that being a relative pronoun of nature is the subject of verb makes. 28-that will be spread, that being a relative pronoun of talent is the subject of verb will be spread. 29- and that must be spread, that being a relative pronoun of talents is the subject of verb must bedspread. 30- king means large, wide, immense. 31- ritzy means gentle. 32- graces is the subject of verb will make. 33- joint is a qualificative adjective of graces. 34- prior means important. 35-vim means vigor, vitality. 36 well-paid means expensive and sophisticated. 37- reversed means upside down. 38-getting on means advancing. 39-not to have made him, him replaces son. 40-chasuble means robe of priests and pastors. 41-straight is an adverb. 42-strength means safety, secureness.. 43-she is the subject of verbs attracts, sees, makes, drives, enchants, captivates. 44-meant means cheap, inferior.45-parents is the subject of verb accept. 46- amazed is an adjective past participle of parents. 47- flame means splendor. 48-boy means son. 49the dots of suspension replace them. 60-cham means false and not genuine. 52-thought means remembrance in the improper sense. 52- cheers means happiness. 53- man is the subject of verbs goes, unloads and asks. 54- astounded is an adjective past participle of man. 55- informant means tutor. 56- gallant is the subject of verb runs. 57-he quickens through him, him replaces Pan.58- aver means declare. 59-the dots of suspension replacesyouy.60-troubled is a qualificative adjective of Mick. 61- gaunt means sexy. 62- waken means enliven. 64- leal means legal. 64-hilarity means gaiety, happiness. 65-creditors is the subject of verbs could see and will agree. 66- she is the subject of verbs earns, has and makes 67-so quick is an adverb.

D

No 25

Great artist

I

O you, super star! Women adore you
As a god precisely because this is
A man, a man quite visible and due,
A man who has eyes for watching ladies,
A tongue for talking to them, both hands for
Playing the guitar, a crowd of other
Qualities quite human, that are encore
Specially appreciated by nicer..........1

II

Ah! Super star! You think up of having certain
Ideas, certain opinions, a little
Of reason, and you believe that we then
Will tolerate it? What! Mister Jacktel,
You have the ear of kings and of presidents
Who listen you, who apprehend you, who love
You, who hug you, who enjoy your amusements,

III

Who love you, who coddle you, who shower
Honors and gifts upon you and you do
Not find that it is not enough ever
As that. Not happy to then reign in true

And absolute master on their senses,
To shake them, to jostle them, to make them
Jump, dance, laugh, shed in tears to your ease
Or your whim as the puppets protem2,

IV

You want to teach them, to enlighten,
To instruct them, to infiltrate a ray
Of the spirit in their heads, ah! Today,
After that nice stroke what does it happen?
Some people took you by the armand put
You out, by telling you: get out, chosen
Beggar that wants to be sensed, I think about!

V

That wants to have ideas! And now, you are
In the streets without a penny, without
Knowing where to go, you become bizarre.
O star! That will learn to remain, no doubt,
Such as God created you, you are quite
Ashamed to see you treated as a poet,
Instead of magnificent palace that right3
Opens up, my friend, to welcome you yet,

VI

Instead of the sumptuous tables where
No one dares taking place before you, then
Instead of awes that one gives you, to scare
Not to have a splendid plan, not to win
A piece of bread. So much the worse for you!
Why were not you discreet? Why are you greedy,
Ambitious? Alas! No one was too
Kind toward this man who procures money,

Vii

Nevertheless, the American women
Were not generous to this eminent
Man who procured so many uses. Then
He is always noble and jubilant,
Always well-versed and open, no one can
Paint him and describe him with more wisdom,
To ornament him with more resplendent
Elegance that he is now at random.

1-the dots of suspension replace women. 2-protem is an adverb and means temporarily. 3-right is an adverb. 4-uses means possessions.

No 26

United States

I

The harmony of your admirable aspects
Always pure and original calls poetry;
It would be inspire me; and such is the art with which
The different tools employed, that all feel effects,
That all are expected, that all are melted, only
In a perfect unity quite very rich,

II

O United States! You have in the character
So much sweetness and so much firmness, with so much
Genius, you have led the existence the most
Joyous and brilliant. You know that ahead the master1
Or lofty man that it is not granted to touch,
To speak, to have ideas, intelligence almost,

III

When the harmony never casts a gloom upon
By its dissonances the transparent purity
Of a melody that flows like a clear river.
That keeps this calm and serene life that you pass on.
The style, this is you! I contemplate your dainty
Aspect an aspect quite calm, reposed, and nicer;

V

Those wonderful and majestuous ornaments
Whose never either the wind or the rain have not
Defrozen a unique buckle, let us listen
These melodious, limpid and so equal chants,
And tell me if the misfortune, suffering, lot,
Desire, worry, disappointment, have left often

VI

An only trace in the florescence of your honest
Aspect in the continual smiling
Of your happy spirit. Do not you find this sky
Without clouds that, is your unspoiled and manifest,
Bliss, disconcert further and cool you're well-wishing?
You wish all human beings should lead a life so high.

VII

And do not you feel well otherwise attired through
The works the most human where you find back your joys
And your pains, where you feel that world lived from your life,
Happy from your happiness, really led a true
Style from your style, full of hope and woe, and annoys
As you? Those who live in you find that you are so rife.

VIII

The everlasting beatitude is a fruit
Of the other world; the other world, this is you;
That loses so many of its tastes for being
Transplanted in this one. Where is your charming flute
For charming it, o America! You are true
And unable to feel other thing than giving 3.

1-master is written at the singular because of the rhyme.
2-chrystalline means transparent. 3-giving means generosity.

No 27

Islamic regiment

I

O Islamic followers! Dare sharing to kings,
To presidents, to diplomats, and to the world
Your hates, your crimes, your antipathies, your unthinkings;
Dare bending you in front of your abyss quite so curled
All those men1 of pride
And of vanity, who,
Forgetting that good side
Of Muhammad who too
Modest, wise and honest,
That he had no place where
Resting his egoist
Mind on the so unfair
Human conditions, pride themselves insolently
On the criminality. I dare helping you
To tear up the veil that covers your ordinary
Sights; all worldwide troubles come from leaders quite undue.

II

I dare telling you that we do not satisfy
At your divine laws that beget hostilities,
Conflicts, that try to impose on the world your sly
Doctrine and the other idiosyncrasies.
I compel you to then
Make the laws that command

The love; this is even
To say: sweetness, demand2,
Humility, blessing,
Indulgence, abstinence,
That without remaining
Love, this so intense
Necessary constituent of this religion,
All what they can do for the salvation is wasted.
If you are Muslims or an army of legion,
If you are soul, dare showing as Muslims well-bred.

III

O Muslims! I dare telling you that this honor,
This nobleness, those titles that they confiscate
On the virtue, that those wealth whose they thus offer
You or show you, are many inappropriate
Crimes to the God's eyes who
Made all the men brothers,
Cannot have among you
Other better manners
Or other distinctions
That those ones of merit,
Of virtue, of devotion,
And of love; then permit
To tell you that the earth is the domain of God
And belongs to all of us indistinctly. For
If in the share of common domain the parts quite odd
May not be equal as we pretended encore,

IV

It is necessary that certain persons have
The least in order that the earth is proportioned
To the needs of each one, and not counted on grave

And vain titles or in step with faith thus mentioned.
We the pagans who are
Rich do many charities
To profits of poor, so far,
Who do not love clashes,
War and conflicts! I dare
Telling you the Muslims,
The Islamists, the fair
Imams about their vims3,
The religious ministers, the preachers, that4 God
Did not create us richer or poorer the ones more
Than the others; we all children his children not clod,
That5 he loves with an equipoten6 love encore;

V

And his paternal God suffers more to see that,
Whereas in America all are joy and parties,
Elsewhere all are miseries and mourning's a lot;
He7 puts no race of color above other races;
He is not a racist.
Dare calling you Muslim!
Go a true islamist
Is above all the brims
Of fears, of all cowardice,
Of all weakness. He thence
Runs with joy, sacrifice
Ahead the pursuance8;
A true Muslim supposes to have the love in
His heart, not to offer himself to the suicide;
This is not the faith, this is the ignorance. Then
Now, this you who scatter everywhere homicide.

VI

What is the use of achieving those famous studies
Of Koran, out of which man becomes ignorant
And deraisonable, to do with your sages!
They learn you to turn, to elude all important
Laws of the Gospel, to
To then substitute it
Of others the most due,
The most suitable or fit
To your interests and aims,
To twist sense the clearest,
The simplest to your frames9,
For fitting it to your slighted10
Minds, to cover with a sainted appearance
Your darker heinous crimes, your coward offense against
The freedom and the life of people. Today, whence
The Koran is in all hands quite sensed or unsensed.

VII

Each one might read that the love, the only love,
Infinite and limitless, is all the religion;
There are only heretics, there only pagans of
There that those who become stranger with the region
Of the love. The only
That distinguishes
Children of God truly
With children of Bogeys11,
This is the love; only
Without love all what you
Do for the setting free12
Is useless; only by consequence the selfish,
The proud, the intolerant, the trouble-makers,
Imams, clericals or preachers are not the godish
Children, but they are only members of monsters;

VIII

Only the persecutions, the diatribes and
The political and religious vengeance is
The inspirations of the hell; the hates of fanned13
Nation to nation is anti-religious, far
From human conception;
Since all men are brothers;
War itself, contention
Are for impure manner 14s.
O madmen! Do you have
The first idea of this
Religion so grave
Whose you make yourselves amiss
Disciple! This is a mistake of believing
That God intervenes in the bloody debate15
Of mortals; but this is a mistake of being
Pardonable to the one who is questioned straight16
On what he thought about
The preachers the most
Followed of his time. Out
Of here, there is almost
No freedom. Islamists
Blessing flags of their
Rules with iron hands17, fists18
Instead of praying their
God to change their hearts or to send an angel
Of exterminator who can kill those who walk
In front of their regiments that like to murder people.
Imam does not plead the godly causes in his talk.
1-men is the subject of verb themselves. 2-demand means essentiality.
3-vim means zeals. 4-that God did not create, that being a
conjunctive pronoun is the complement of direct object of verb
dare telling. 5- that he loves with, that being a conjunctive pronoun
is the subject of verb dare telling. 6equipoten means equal. 7-he

puts no race, he replaces God. 8-persuance means persecution.. 9-frames means state of mind. 10-slightest means narrowest. 11-Bogeys means Satan or demon. 12-setting free is an expression that means salvation. 13- fanned is a qualificative of nation and means fanatic and extremist. 14-manners means behaviors. 15- debate is written at the singular because of the rhyme. 16- straight is an adverb. 17-rules with iron hands is a locution that means regiment. 18- rule with iron fists is a locution that means regiment

No 28

United States

I

O United States! If you had
Less rights to my everlasting
Thanks, if you were not the odd
Land where the most gratifying
Years of my life pass, in middle
Of a worthy society,
At the same time reputable,
Amiable and neighborly,
Whose the remembrance or keepsake
Would be dear to me without fake.

II

If I could bear a grudge against
You after favors whose you truly
Gratified me, the so enhanced
Honors that you showered upon me,
The retation that you gave
Me, I would wish you that your land
Would remain the land of the brave
Poets. All men who enlightened
In favor of you or against you
Are welcome on your so due ,..........1 ;
Speak about love and charity
Are the blessed voices for you.

III

All the voices that talk to you
About the love and charity
Are the blessed voices for you. Too
According to your so worthy
Marvels, I know nothing, and then
I am nothing less than a saphead2,
A lunatic, and not even
A stranger. A dunderheaded3,
That could be; but I remain
And well remain honest and sane.

IV

It is not given to all men
To be also scholarly than
Voltaire and Rousseau who even
Do not want at all cost that faith then
Is less a science than a virtue,
Less the fruit of human reason
Than of grace. If I was a true
Preacher without thought of treason,
After tomorrow there would be
No heads in immense assembly;

V

I would have to a medicine,
So that there were no sick patients
In the hospital. With routine,
I know that the lie would not be
More advantageous than truth for
Me. Nothing cannot stop really
America in the so fore4
Mission that it asserts itself

To do, because it has the self.
1-the dot of suspension replace land. 2-sahead means
fool. 3-dunderheaded, 4- that could be, that being
demonstrative pronoun is the subject of verb could be.
4- fore is a qualificative of mission and means first,

No 29

Baseness

I

How much baseness for succeeding in?
You must display yourself, not such as
You are, such as they wish you to be. Then,
Baseness of adulation, whereas
They incense and
They just adore......1
That we then tend
To despise more!
Baseness of cowardice, you must know
How to endure the dislikes, to eat
Up the wastes, to receive them comme il faut2
As blessings on the divine pulpit!

II

Baseness of dissimilation, not
To have the feeling in self, and then
To think only by others as jot!
Baseness of dissoluteness, even
To become great
Partners, maybe
The delegate4
Of zealotry5
Of those to whom you depend! At last,
Baseness of hypocrisy, to more

Borrow the appearance of past
Pity, to play honest man for.......6

III

O you who dream only the mites and
Poke, whose the life arrives to flatter
The passions from those whose we thus tend
To expect something; you who slaughter
The truth at your
Prejudices,
Who turn off encore
The lambencies7
Of Gospel, who8, by fear of depleasing,
Make you everywhere the pillars of
Tyranny, who9 are not opposing
To those who have audacity as you shove

IV

Of combatting you only by arms
Of injustice and of violence,
For dare telling you the true gendarmes
Or the ministers of an immense
Religion of peace
And love. Reader,
I do not miss
Anything ever!
This is not to you, that is aimed at
The time of men that I accuse is
Far from us, and I therefore do not
Implyto those who, with great ease,
Read me with any
Frightful passion
That set presently

The real ration
Of misery
Of word. You all are, I am certain,
Full of zeal and of devotion for
The good. The egoism, often
This empoioned root is the encore
Disturbance and
All the crimes, thence
Has no sogrand
Push on my sense
Or on my heart. The selfishness is
The plague of love. And you, are not you
Religious? Are not you the keys
Of love, sweetness, full of zeal for truth?

V

This is not you who are going to
Know me in the mosque or the church
That I trace. For this isnot you who
Hate me, who curse me and who just search
To then weigh me
Down by your wraths,
Who thus carry
Out your own scaths10,
Your threats, your vengeances on me, who
Pierce me with your spiteful looks, and then
With your traits of flame soaked11 in a new
Ink, who pursue to bother me even
In front of great
Lords of world. Whence
I depend, straight
To whom I thence
Dare telling truth. The world is a nice
Vehicle of matter in motions

In step with law, man himself, with no price,
Is a similar machine. Sensations
Just enter him
As motions and
Beget and trim
Our pictures and
Our ideas. Each idea is the start
Of a motion and becomes a deed
Of idea. Every idea does lead
Or moves the body in some degree apart.

1-The dots of suspention replace image or idol. 2-comme ill faut is an adverbial locution and means it should be. 4-delegate is written at the singular because of rhyme. 5-zealotry means passion. 6-the dots of suspension replace succeeding. 7-lambencies means lights. 8-who, by fear of depleasing, who being a relative pronoun of you is the subject of verb make. 9-who are not opposing, who being a relative pronoun of you is the subject of verb are opposing. 10-scaths means rancors. 11-soaked is an adjective past participle of ink.

No 30

Truth

I

Only by the truth a man is great.
Betraying truth, this is to vitiate
Oneself. You see mit better than anybody;
You, religious, diplomats, are truly
Appealed to tell
The truth even
To the grave hell.
Not you who then
Take away the bread from my proper hand,
By abusing against me your command.
Alas! If you knew what I suffer,
What I have suffered, if you knew the better
Fights that I had
Delivered, the bad
Struggles that I
Sustained, the high
Force of will whose I need for resisting
To despair, you will be understanding
It before hurling the anathema.
If you see yourself in the replical
Of egoists
And extremists,
This is not my
Fault. I thus try

To describe the horrors of past, only
For consoling you by this very
Hour, and to make you inhale the future
With a special attraction or feature.

II

That does not hinder me to find that Steve
Had reason when he told: "Do not believe
To be either muslims or Christians or
Judaists, but worship a God quite more
Good and clement.
The western states
Did their excellent
Works, made good estates3.
After two hundred years of massacre4
And lootings, in hands of the commander-
In- chief of stuntman the power wholly
Returned. Their beaten enemies, truly
Were only his
Humble valets,
Bended5 at his
Whims or maggots,
And also at obedience the most
Servile, ready at all the uttermost
Complaisanc4e, at all the baseness,
At all the heinous crimes that he did please
In master to
Impose them, right6
To make them too
Kneel day and night
Ahead his will, ahead his passions and
Ahead his whims,____ much happy and much grand
To debase himself for just a title,
A dignity, any favor so vital;

III

To require the honors at the expense
Of honor, with pride the public remembrance7
Of their debaseness, of their ignominy.
The president reconquered all his wee
Power, but crow
Always moaned in
The servitude.
The crowd is then
Reduced to the frightful misery
By lucky commander-in-chief and fancy
Prodigalities of regent, people
To the struggle were dying by the total
Extreme hungers
Thousands of true
Burghers, voters,
Citizens, too
Victims of despotism and intolerance,
Saw themselves all the days cruelly thence
Tore away from bosom of their families
For being jailed in the frightful houses
Of detention
Only God then
Knows their pretention
And what certain
Prisoners got to suffer from horrihble
State of jails at that time! For quite a terrible
Bed a bit of dam straw, crowded by insects,
Whose the sleep would never approche, no prospects.
1-replica means mirror in the improper sense 3-estates means
social studied. 5- bended being an adjective past participle of
enemies. 6-right is an adverb. 7-remembrace means token

Opinion

I

The opinion, daughter_____ of the press, does commence
Its reign. To the brilliant_____ products of imaging
Power1 will put2 over_____ the words of influence.
The search for evident_____ truth on everything
Will become workaday3_____ of poets and savants.
Destroying the error_____ prejudices, abuses;
Just reducing at bay_____ the fans or adherents
And absolute power4;_____broadcasting the science;

II

That is the work that_____ is the use of ending5.
All, until the disputes _____quite theological,
Are going to compete_____ the whole affrachisings6
Of human attitudes _____ or the corporal7
Spirits. Thought is only_____ a second wind, but this
Second wind moves the world. _____Be courageous, according
As the philosophy_____ spirit enters amiss8
Social prison so wirled. _____Be brave and unbending;

III

You will hear edifice_____ cracking down everywhere,
And the humanity_____ will get out of it free
And radious with bliss, _____ will become young and fair

By this wind normally_____ come9 from new happy
World. Those narrow-minded__ leaders make no yielding
To the spirit of time, _____ who see only their own
Benefit, who ahead_____ consult only their fitting
Selfishness, and meantime____pushed
country in a unknown......10 ;

IV

Except only that folk,_____ this unchained lion, stirs
A little air of breath_____ of their lung, for seeing
Them11 shakinglike they choke___and running away as hares
So shy, leaving as death_____ the king exposed by hulking12
Dangers, forced to oppose_____ a calm face to the brim
Vociferations that_____ besiege him, to naked
Swords that it does expose, _____ sees returned against his grim
Chest. Infamous and fat_____ traitors very ill-bred,

V

Who13 went to solicit_____ against their country, who14
Went to attract civil_____ war on the sorer! Heinous
Egoistsquite unfit, _____ who15, rather thanto yield too
The good grace to the real, ___ mighty torrentof cuss16
Ideas, rather than to_____ make generous surrender17
Of what they injustly_____possessed, rather than to
Admit at what the true_____ equity, the honor,
Respect, humanity,_____ reason, would like to
Precipitate country_____in all kind of misfortune18!
They have eyes for not seeing, __ ears for not hearing. Too,
Were they deaf really_____ to this terrible tune
Or voice, whose the frowning___ accent made ocean blue
Move back, to this voice that____ rose scaring everywhere,
That let them really know_____ that a change became so
Necessary and pat, _____ that the time quite so fair

Occurred to bring the flow_____ violence down comme il faut19,
That nothing could stop_____ that change to accomplish?
They put themselves in the top____ to do the devilish..........20

VI

Were they truly deaf to_____ this much formidable
Voice, that resounded from_____North to the South, to this
Moaning wind, to this new_____thunderbolt, to this able
Storm, that whispered to some___ ears of the peopulace
These electrical words._____ They eat, drink, and enjoy;
They taste all joys, all nice_____ pleasures, all glutonies;
They roll as human-birds_____ in the silk, gold as toy;
They sleep in the precise _____ beds of cedar; their ideas,
When it is the usage _____of their rests, are occupied
Only by the way whose_____ they will be able to
Vary nice privilege _____of their possessions, pride;
So to rewachas the snooze_____ without boredom the true
End of day. By waiting _____ the people in the old
Cloth works, plow, scatter, mow,___ in prey to the sun, to
The hail; they are brooking, _____ they exhaust, they then hold
Or they lavish their flow _____life by thousand ways, too
For providing royal_____ bankets, for satisfying
Voracious appetites_____ of so many starved dinner
Guests. Those are their formal_____qualities, their granting
Prvileges, their rights_____for living without ever
Nothing to do like that_____at the expense of people
Who are born to work at _____ their place with no title.
1-imaging power means imagination. 2-put over means succeed.
3-workaday uses as a common noun and means occupation.
4- absolute power means tyranny. 5- ending means accomplish.
6- affranchising means emancipation. 7-corporal means human.
8- remissmeans neglected. 9-come is an adjective past participleof
wind. 10-the dots of suspension replace way. 11-for seeing them
shaking, them replce leaders. 12-hulking means big. 13-who

went to solicit, who being a relaive pronoun is the subject of verb went. 14-who went to attract, who being a relative oronoun of traitors is the subject of verb went. 15-who, rather than to yield, who being a relative pronoun of traitors is the subject of verb like. 16- cuss uses as a qualificativ4e adjective of ideas. 17-surrendermeansabadonment. 18-misfortune is written at the singular because the rhyme. 19- comme il faut, is an expression that means as it should be. 20-theb dots of suspensionreplaced acts.

No 32

Ambition

The ambitious is never satisfied.
Alas! All the things
Are only vanity. Bliss does reside
Neither in richstandings
Nor in the splendors; it is entirely
In our heart. We carry
In us, if weknow to drink it truly,
The cup of jollity1.
The happiness, this nectar makes the sweetnest,
kind of pinks of flowers,
Freshly hatched by the clear rivers. I guest
That the sky thus simpers2-
at the nature; the true crowned with flowers
and with verdure sway by
the puff of morning with powers.
Come to stroll11 with me on high
Silvery sands, on the grass in bloom. Then
Come to the sterling spring
To quench your heart. What begging to even
Amuse an admiring
Woman who is not so amusable.
She liked to taste splendors,
She finds that this is a unlikeable
Wine. From part of kissers4,
She would like to remove them5, but it is
Too late. Without a dense

Discrimination the man would with ease
Has more intelligence,
More talents, more virtuyes, the one who by
His nature, resemble
The most to God, and humbles himself by
A so insensible
Gradation and quite well in harmony
With system of nature
Would not give ride to any anarchy,
To any disorder.
Each one would be at his place, in milieu
That suits him. He is free
From all constraint, as the bees among new
Flowers, as the pretty
Swallows in the fields of the air, as lions
On the top of Atlas.
For amusing herself with her chagrins
Quite domestic, she thus
Occupies her heart and her mind to high
Love those who then suffer.
She relieves the load of her splendor by
The charity. Further,
It should better relieve the poor people
Today. It is quite fai
That those poor live by you in principle,
Since they have been so bare6
By you. And you pretend to be human7,
For we all are the men
Of ambition and of intolerance, who8 then
Forget very often
The sweetness and humankind are only
Weapons whose God permit
Them to use, who9 thus torturesthe body
For converting a bit

The soul, and who10 let drop the tears with blood,
Instead of ignoring
The ones and of sparing others. With bud
Of emancipating:
The satisfaction that vengeancegives you
Lasts only a little
Time, but this one that the clemency too
Gives you is esternal.

1-jolity means bliss, felicity. 2-simpers means smiles. 3-stroll means take a walk. 4- poart of kissers is a locution that means lips, mouth. 5-to remove them, them replaces splendors. 6-bare means deprived, ruined. 7-human means humane. 8who then forget, who being a relative pronoun of men is the subject of verb forget. 9-and who tortures the body, who being a relative pronounof God is the subject of verbtortures. 10-who let drop the tears with blood, who being a relative pronoun of God is the subject of verb let drop

No 33

Friendly Tummy

I

I therefore cannot stop me
To report a word so bold,
Excellent from a baby1
Woman of thirty years old,
Who, having caused some pretty
Fret to man that she did hold
Or loved, were punished hardly.

II

The lover, who by his nature
Of poet, thought he grew up
With some level or mature
Ken2 above the men like a pup3,
Wanted to then decipher
His vengeance as a tup4
By saying this verse: "The pleasure
Of gods makes the vengeance up"

III

Another day he hardly
Outraged her with the unfair
Suspicion; she suddenly
Ended the worst blame by those scare

Words: "This is to revenge me.
There is only gods who share
The vengeance. I am only
A poor, to god is my prayer;

IV

A destitute woman who
Cannot die with worries, prays
God for you." Tummy, then too
Passionate, tender, did daze
To have merited such a true
Woman who truly did praise
Him, but Loodmillard quite due
Is this one who does amaze 5

V

Nevertheless, among
All his girlfriends Loodmillard
Is this one that he loved so long.
In a perilous and hard
Occasion he wrote this strong
Note that in her heart she did guard:
"if I am beaten, along,
You know me enough to regard
That I will never be wrong
Of flee; but my last soft or hard
Thought will be to God, along
Before last for you a card.

VI

Tummy saw a night that she
Fixedly looked at a star
And told her: "Do not much see

It, my dear, I cannot so far
Give it to you." At any
Rate a thing that we afar
Cannot pass under steady
Silence, for as a nice star
She really honors Tummy,
But she does not loss him so far.

VII

Tummy has employed only
The patience, the favors
And the skills for normally
Bringing back the brainpowers
That factions seduced truly.
A king told: "Wise characters6
Are as bright7 apothecary
Who composes counteracters8
Quite excellent and makes truly
Of theriac with the vipers
From poisons so rickety9
And so dangerous as monzers10.

VIII

Such was his bounty that never either
The hate or the vengeance had any right
To entry in his heart, and that ever
He forgave, considering as a quite
Great harm of being forced to punish. Then
This kindness that gave him, with his friends, thence
The courtesy the sweetness and open,
Toward those people, the benevolence
The most tender; with his nobles, the most
Touching quality; there is what lifts him,

As much as his heroism almost
Unequalled, as much as his clever and prim11
Politic, above all kings and presidents
On-earth; there is what conciles forever generous
Hearts; there is what then fixes his penchants
And love that he has for Loodmillard thus.

1-baby means young in the improper sense. 2-ken means experience. 3-pups dog. 4-tup means male sheep. 5-hardly means cruelly 5- the dots of suspension replace him. 6-characters means people. 7-bright means clever, skillful. 8-couteracters means antidotes. 9-rickety means dangerous. 10-monzers means virulence. 11- pim means precise.

No 34

Tender-heartedness

I

Michael, at the fight of Middle East, the only
Where he dared appearing,
Listening the whistle of bullets, gentlely
Asked his so wonting
Confessor what he thought of this music so sad.
He answered: "I find it quite
Very disagreeable." __And me also, had
Replied explicit
Michael: "My father was a man so comical
To take so much pleasure
In it." He shook with terror all tune of battle,
And this resolves never
To assist in his life such a feast. Eady,
One of those unlucky
Victims, dared coming near to the king, and really
Told him: "May you, lord, be
Witness of such a barbarity without goaning?
He answered cooly: "Thence,
If my son, Michael, was suspect of free thinking,
I would give up him, whence
I am telling you. My horror is such for you
And for your fellow-men;
If I was short of torturers, I would use too
Myself as hangman1.

II

As for the prince, Michael, the whistle of the shots2
Affected him, his strong
Valiancy tested by the thousand combats,
Then does not go along
With the least doubt in the respect. The world was so
Powerful voice that then
Proclaimedheroism of Tummy. Apropos,
The democrats often
Did not stop deploringthe harms of civil war.
He shook to see brothers
Armed against brothers, friends against friends. He therefore
Worried about the futures
Of the world, to which the victory should be
Always fatal. The prince
Told: "lord, if it advantageous to my lovely
People that I will thence
Possess the crown, promote my cause, and then protect
My arms; if not, kill me,
And that my death is the last term of incorrect
Wars that destroy my country."

III

Also the administration and the vigor
That procured made him
A celestial shield against which all the stronger
Spirit of hell quite grim
Came to disappear. I raised it up to God
The dandy victory
Of my cause, because he pretended to be a glad
Christian. Consequently,
He rejected all the ideas of the cruel
Reprisals toward his strong

Enemies; he gave an absolute refusal
At all the crimes quite wrong.
The prince justified the slogan that he even
Took at exact title.
He was always sincere to his character, then
In which the vital
Nations desiered to recognize the amazing
Prince who were quite so strong
Among them, who was brightened up by his fitting
Words all those who were along
With him, who electrified them by some true
Projections of s soul
Quite lively and of a generous heart, and who3
Were at same time of a whole
Man of intelligence and of a hero, and
Who4 were always smiling,
Always affable, always franc, open and grand,
And always well-pleasing.

IV

The prince has carried all his subjects in his heart,
And loved to visit huts
Of peasants, to share his bread, to toast the smart
Glasses with them, and juts;
He kept himself informed with bounty of his state,
Or his predicaments
And of his ressources; he did gaily relate
All his proper contents
With his family; he played gladly with his children.
Let the tears and secret
Despair of the misery of will come to then
Reproach him for the set
Misfortunes or faults. What a majestic figure!
Who would not feel his heart

Attracted through him? Who would not love this stronger
Prince? He was sweet and tart.

1-hangman means executioner. 2-shots means bullet. 3-who were at
same time, who being a relative pronoun of those is the subject of verb
Were. 4-who were always smiling, who being a relative
pronoun of those is the subject of verb were.

America

I

Do you like sweet things? Very good, I will tell you
Some truths, I esteem in your finest genius
That the age bore; I admire you as a true
Poetry, I also love you as a prose. Thus,
Never a country before
You had a shape so living,
A taste quite so sure and more
Delicate. You are charming
In conversation; you know
How to amuse and to teach
At the same time. You are so
Seductive country so rich
That I know. I came too late, I do not regret
It, for I live in you. You encourage yourself
To seduce tourists because you are in vedette
Your smile and the grace of your aspect as a pelf,
Added to the charm of your
Conversation and music
Of your voice, leads me to more
Offer you my full but civic
Love. O nice land! You spoil me
By returning my love in kind!
You who passed through many
Arms of talents, and thus find

A new experience and happiness in my
Devotion. You are tired of soulless love, you hence
Aspire to begin with me a pure and high
Life. You bought me from several issues, free me thence.

II

You invite me to share your wealth. You gave me
A beautiful wife who understands me and who
Accepts me for who I am. And I normally
Realized that I sinned by disertingher, and you
Tought me wisdom in begging
Her forgiveness; she accepted,
But spurned2 to be forgetting.
She normally decided
To atome for meandering
Morals of our past by best.2
Living her remaining
Years in contenance. My highest
Propensity to love in a corrupted youth
Takes altogether a spiritual direction.
America seems to desire with the truth
That one sex may by the senses perceive perfection,
Kindness, beauty in other.
And so, by the sight of this girl,
And by my strong love for her,
A new world of beauty, of pearl,
Of excellence did uncover
To me. For I never lost
That world; one woman after
Another stirred my so just
And sensitive spirit, always with reverence
As well as desire, at the age of fifty-nine
I fell more in love with my wife in a stable sense.
For a while I was too awed to speak to the fine......3

III

It is a pleasant sensation when a new
Passion begins to stir in us before the old
One is quite extinct. When the sun is sitting, too
One likes to see the moon rising the opposite cold
Side. Since that day, sun, moon, and
Stars can go calmy about
Their business, but I am bland4
And conscious neither about
Day nor about night, and whole
World around me is fading
Away. I have no more droll
Prayers to say excluding5
To my nice wife and to you, o America!
I am more sentimental, more given to teards
And gashing words and self-commiseration. Ah,
Your name is uttered in reverence by those dears
Of adoring lips! I found
In you a sedative for
Passion; and a profound,
Free, wide view over more
Sensible and moral world
Seemed to open before me.
You are kindly and so pearled,
I praise youwith all your free
Works.o America! You are not wise either
Quiet or wild, but you are a beauty, a marvel,
A lifestyle, an open mind, a kind heart,
And you are everything that makes the integral
World live comfortable; you art a superb art.

IV

I am sensible of feeling an attractive
Power of gentlest kind in you. For you grow
Into the habit of seeing each other; active
You are! You are now useful to each other. Oh!
An irresistible longing
Dominates the world, so quickly
That can rise a respecting
Fever, blown up by sympathy
Of a poet. I tried hard
To be frank to you; I tried
Sometimes to have a regard
For other coutries that died..
But I have no taste for vulgarity. Therefore
I idealizeyou as a sacred mystery
To be approached with the reverence. Furthermore,
Your conversation is brilliant, exemplary;
Your language is very warm
And powerful, but your feelings
Are swayed by love, hate and storm.
You have marvelous bearings
Of the highest beauty. Then
Your voice is gentle and repressed.
No one can fail to often
Mark on your face quite so blessed:
Seriousness, gentleness kindiliness, virtue,
And profound sensibility. You are very
Pious, with a so affecting and almost too
Ecstatic elevation of soul and sturdy.

V

From exquisite carriage and your almost
Professional skill in dancing one would hardly
Infern tranquil moonlight that fills your heart with most
Peace. When I came here, you are still ailing from truly
Repeated largess, and then
Your sense of superpower
Enters into thew open-
Mindedness of your temper.
You are something new in my
Rosary of marvels; and
Nonetheless you are a high
Aristocrat, in whom grand
And fine manners seem inborn. I see you as enshrined
In nobility. It was one result of your vast
Community relationship that you assigned
To transmit to me the manners of your steadfast,
And schooled me in self-possession,
Moderation, courtesy.
You are grateful for my passion
As restoring my urgency
In life, but accept it as
Land of breeding receives full
Honor from a man who has
Been fifty-eight- your old brimful
Than you, as the hold man pains with an eager
Spirit seeking the experience and fulfillment.
Your beauties has a wondrous effect or matter
Upon me. There are no words for it, I resent.

No 36

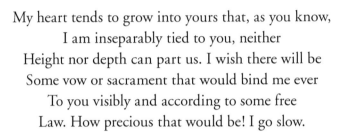

My heart tends to grow into yours that, as you know,
I am inseparably tied to you, neither
Height nor depth can part us. I wish there will be
Some vow or sacrament that would bind me ever
To you visibly and according to some free
Law. How precious that would be! I go slow.

II

My novitiate is surely long enough for
Me to take all due thoughts. The Americans have
The cords that they bind about their arms in the act
Of prayer. I thus bind about my arm your save1
Cords when I address my prayer to you, attract
You to impart to me your kindness, patience, and,more.

III

I enjoy to repeat to you that I love you,
That your assurance that you are indeed taking
Pleasure in my love renews the joy of my life.
I have borne much in silence, but I am having
Desired nothing more than our relationship
Might take a form over which no case could have few.......2

IV

If that cannot be, I would not dwell where you are,
But rather be alone in this world that I now
Go forth. I admire your mind so rapturously,
Having never met such brilliance in sill-somehow
Women that I went to ypou everyday, really
Paid your compliments that seemed to restore your bizarre 4

V

You have me pampered with every form of womanly
Solicitude. Yourself somewhat masculine, whence
You are not displeased by my almost tender
Delicacy. Unable to see me, you thence
Could moldthe image close of me to the desire
Of your heart, and you fall in love with that copy5.

VI

Able to see me, I could never forget you
And your physical helpfulness. When I went back
To Florida, you wrote me some letters almost
As warmth with the devotion ad those of shakwack5
To tim, and written in fine prose so that she most
To Tim, written as a fine prose that age could show too.

VII

My replies tried to check your elevation; then
You shivered at the thought of what the New-Yorkers
Would do with such a juicy morsel of satire.
You suffered my reproofs, reaffirmed your desires
And your love, agreed to its friendshid quite entire,
But assumed me that in New- York friendship is often
Deeper and stronger than love. I belong to you

More than myself. I wish I could send you my soul
Instead of a letter. I would willingly give
Up years of my life to be sure of being whole
And alive when I come back to New-York active7
This is the highest praiuse I could offer you,

VIII

I come back to New-York and you thetrefore await
Me with virginal excitement. At last, no sea
Divides us. I cannot make myself believe that
A man of my importance could naturally
Leave everything to come back to your splendid flat7.
It is absurb, but I am enchanted and feel great.

IX

It is not a dream, I know I am awake; then
I shall see you today. You sent your car for me,
I caome to you at once. I therefore promise to
Gladden you with my presence and to normally
Sadden you my cautions. When I had gone to new
Florida, you thought of my returning often
To New _York. The collapse of your romance darkened
The mporal pessimism of a lover who
Missed the colors of life but its shallows
And depth. Even in blindness you could see hold in view
Through all the gallant surfacesto the egos
Or indefatigable selfishness of grand.........9

X

I begins by feeling boring with her in spite
Of my loving efforts, I return to Florida.
My ex-lover told her friend: "My poor tutor, have
You met only monsters, crocodiles? As for me,ah,

I see only fools, idiots, liars, so grave,
Envious, sometimes perfidious men not wight10.

XI

"everyone I see here dries up my heart, I find
No virtue, no sincerity, no simplicity
In anyone." From Florida, I keep calling
Her. One day she indeed told me:" I normally
Continue my suppers, usually evening
A week, and often drive out, if only behind
To avpoid boredom of days as dark as the nights."
At last she, who had learned to hate life, stopped clunching
It, and reconciled herself to death. The illness
That plagues fifty-six years old woman quite clinging11
Had mounted and combined, and she feltthe weakness
To fight a lover. She sent me her last notes with no wights.

XII

"I am worse and I cannot think that this condition
Means anything but the end. I am not so strong
Enough to be frightened, an as I am not to
See you again I have nothing to bite my tongue13.
Amuse yourself, my friend, as well as you can. Do
Not distress yourself about my own condition.
You will normally regret me, for one is glad
To know that one is loved. Since she did, I am still sad.
1-save uses as a qualificative adjective of cords. 2-the dots of
suspension replace power. 4-the dots of suspension replace
golden day. 5-copy means picture. 6-shakwack means woman.
7- active being a qualificative adjective of New-York is placed
after the common noun because of rhyme. 8-flat means
apartment in the commun noun. 1-the dots of suspension
replace self. 10-wight means brave. 11- wights means force.

No 37

Return of tenderness

A lover, to be almost so agreeable,
Must understand how to utter the fine feeling,
To sight forth the soft, the tender, the likable,
The passionate, and his address must be according
To the rules. In the first place he should behold, either,
At the restaurant, in the park, at the movie,
Or some public ceremony, the character1
Of whom he becomes enamored, or else he should be
Nicely introduced to Odette by a pure friend,
And go from her melancholy and so pensive.
He conceals his passion for some time f4rom neatened
Beloved object, but pays several so active
Visits, at which some discourse about gallantry
Never fails to be brought upon the carpet to
Exercise the wits of all the great company.
Whenever he awakes from his dream, I find to love you.....2

II

That speech and that look disarm my excitement,
And produce a return of tenderness that then
Effaces all her guilt. How strange and important
It is to be in love! And that men should be even
Subject to such weakness for those traitesses! Whence
Everyboidy knows imperfection, they are
Nothing but extravagance and improvidence;

Their minds is wicked and their understanding bizarre
And weak; nothing is more frail, nothing is more fake,
   Nothing is more unsteady, and yet, for all that,
   One does everything in the world for the sake
   Of their animals. Ah! Had you but seen her flat3,
You would love her as well as I do. For she came
Everyday to church, and knelt just near me. Therefore,
   She attracted eyes of whole congregation by flame
With which she sent up her prayers to heaven more.

III

   She sighed and graaned very heavily, and at each
      Moment she humbly kinned the earth
As Pope did. When I was going out she would reach
      Or advance before me to offer holy mirth
      And holy water at the door. I made the new
   Presents, but she always modestly would offer
To return me part. At length heaven moved me to
Take her home, since which everything seems to prosper.
   She asked me to become Christian. I made out:
      As I see no character in the life greater
      Or more valuable that to be truly devout,
      Not anything fairerthan fervorof piety;
   So I think nothing more abominable than
      The outside daubing of a pretended zeal,
Than those mountebanks, those devotees in show who then
Make a trade of godliness with certain good will,

IV

"And who4 would purchase honors and reputation
   With hypocritical turning up of the eyes
   Qand affected transports and the exaltation.
I only see that those stars on-earth always rise."

I continue to talk to her:" Misis, will you
Have me be plain with you? I am very so much
Dissatisfied with your way of conduct. I do
Not quarrel with you, but your disposition quite such
Opens to first comer too ready an access
To your heart. You have many lovers whom I see
Besieging you; and my soul cannot thus express
Itself or reconcile itself to this." She really
Felt mad and told me: "Do you
Blame me for attracting lovers? Can I help it
If men find me lovable? When they made a true
Pleasant efforts to see me, I should take a fit 5;

V

Or I should take a stick and drive them out." I said:
"No, it is not a stick that you must indeed use,
But a spiritless yielding and melting ahead
Their vows. I know that your beauty follows, pursues
You everywhere. I determine to live with you
As if you are my wife; but if you know what
I suffer you would pity me. Therefore, my true
Passion naturally reaches such a point that
It even enters with a compassion into
All your interest. When I see how impossible
It is for me to conquer what I feel for you;
I tell myself that you may havesame possible
Difficulty in conquering your preference
To be coquettish, I find myself more likely6
To pity you than to blame you. With no suspense,
You will tell me that a man must a poet to see........7;

VI

"But for my part I feel that there is but one kind
Of love, that8 those who have not felt these delicacies
Of sentiment have never truly loved. Remind
That all things in the world are connected, with ease,
With you in my heart. When I see you, some transports,
An emotion that may be felt but not described,
Take from me all power of reflections, and supports;
I have no longer any eye for your proscribed
Described; I can see only all that you have that
Is lovable. You reveal a world and an art
Almost antipodal. You look like somewhat
You obviously come from a good and so smart
Family; yoiur eyes are clear of fear, unclouded
With even the normal wonderment of the youth;
You have quietly happy and alert to red9
Music of life; and you are brimful with the ruth."

VII

She gives me everyday the pleasure beyond what
I ever know in the possession of her beauty
When I was in the vigor of youth. Every fat
Moment of your life brings me certain lively
Instances of her complacency to my bent10,
And her prudence in regard to my fortune. Then
Her face is to me much more beautiful, decent
When I first saw it, there is no decay in
Any feature which I cannot trace from the very
Instant it was occasioned by certain worried
Concerned for my welfare and interest. Certainly,
The love of a wife is as much above languid
Passion commonly called by that name as the boad
Laughter of buffoons is really mistaken

Or inferior to the elegant and proud
Delight or jollification of gentlemen.

1-character means person in the improper sense. 2-the dots of suspension replace more. 3-flat means apartment. 4-and who would purchase, who being a relative pronoun of mountebanks and devotees. 5-the dots of suspension replace stick. 6-likely means deposed in the improper sense. 7-the dots of suspension replace this. 8- that those who have, that being a cojunctive pronoun is the complement of direct object of verb feel. 9-red means gay. 10- bent means inclination

No 38

I

The world is a machine of matter in motion
According to law, and man himself is
A similar machine. Sensations enter him
As motion, and beget images or ideas,
Each ideas is the beginning of a prim
Motion, and naturally becomes an action
If not impeded by
Another idea. See,
Every idea, however
Abstract, moves the body
In some degree, however
Unseen or very sly1.
The soul and the mind are not immaterial;
They are named for vitual process of body,
Operation of brain. Strength of passion may be
Good and lead to greatness. The one who normally
Has no great passion for powers, wealths, trophy,
Knowledge, or honor that in life are essential,
Cannot possibly have
A great fancy or much
Judgment. To have a weak
Is dullness; to have such
Passions weirdly2 quite thick
And strong is madness; to hve

No desires is to be dead. The human will is
Not free; society is justified in the
Roosting certain actions by calling them virtuous
And rewarding them, and in dismaying3 again
Some actions by calling them wicked or noxious
Punishing them. There are no disparities4.
Here with determinism
These social approvals and
Condemnations are added,
For the good of the band5,
To the motives that ahead
Influenced ethicism.
The world is governedby opinion; government,
Religion, and the moral codes are in larhge part
The manipulation of opinion to reduce
The necessity and area of lion-heart6
Government is necessary and so diffuse7,
Not because man is naturally bad, abhorrent;

II

For the desires and other passions are in
Themselves no sin, but because man is by nature
More individualistic than so social.
As a condition of vier or challenger
Or competition and of so reciprocal
Aggression schecked only by fear, not byet often
By law, we can normally
Visualize that certain
Reciprocal conditions
By observing more often
Many worldwide relations
In our age apparently:
Nations are still for the most part in a state
Of nature, not yet subject to a superimposed

Law or power. In all the times presidents or
Persons of sovereign authority quite posed8,
Because of their independency are in more
Continual jealousies, and in the stae of great
Posture of gladiators,
Having their weapon pointed,
And their eyes fixed,
On one another ahead
Who is not truly commixed,
Their efforts, laagers9,
And guns on the frontiers of their countries and
Continual spies upon their neighbors; which is
A posture of war. Where there are no common powers,
There is no law, there is no injustice; forces
And frauds are in war the cardiunal honors
Or virtues.? Think that individuals and
Kins10 lived in a condition
Of the perpetual war,
Actual or potential,
Every man against man before
The coming of the social
Organization, division11
War consisted not in battle only, but in
A tract of time where the will to contend by fight
Is sufficiently shown. I rejected conjecture12
Of Romamn jurists and Christian philosophers despite
There is, or even the war, a law of nature
In the sense of the laws of right and wrong often
Based upon nature of man
As a so reasonable
Animal; I therefore
Admitted in principle
That man was occasionally
Rational, but even

Saw him rather as a creature of passions above
All; the will to power using reason as a tool
Of desire, and controlled only by fear of force.
Primitive life, this is to sat, life before full
Social organization, was lawless and coarse,
Violent, fearful, nasty, brutishas lion-love.

III

From this hypothetical state of nature, men
Truly emerged by an implicit agreement
One with another to submit to a common
Power. Thius is the social-contract tenent13
Made popular by Rousseau'streatise, but even
Already old. I prefer to think of certain
Social compact as made not
Between ruler and ruled, but
Among the ruled who agreed
To confer all their uncut
Power and strength or their deep
Right to the use of a lot
Of force upon one another, or upon one man,
Or upon one assembly of men. The multitude
So united in one person is called a real
Commonwhealth. This is the generation so good
Of the great Leviathan, or rather than still
Mortal God to which we owe, under the certain
Immortal God, our peace, defense.
Furthermore, this power,
Given him by every man
In the whole empire12,
He had use of much chosen
Power, strenghtand resistence
Conferred on him, that by terror thereof he is
Enabled to form wills of them all to the end

He may use the strength and means of them all,
As he shall naturally think about the bland
Expedient, for their common peace and no brawl13,
For their common defense and for their common release13
1-sly means cover in the improper sense. 2-weirdly means abnormally.
3-dismaying means discouraging. 4-disparities means contradictions.
5-band group. 6-lion-heart means powerful, forceful. 7-diffuse
means spread out. 8- posed mesns set and established. 9-laagers
mens garrison in South Africa. 10-kins means families.. 11-
division means domination in the improper sense. 12- conjecture
means theoryin the improper sense. 13-tenent means theory in
the improper sense.. 14-empire means commonwhealth in the
improper sense. 15- brawl means fight. 16- release means freedom

No 39

Lovely connection

I

My love for you vanishes from my heart
Like smoke and fog and never has any
Existence in my heart. When all your sweet
Words become weak and ungrown in my wee
Heart by your bad comportment quite unneat,
My mind is also weak, not very smart
And undeveloped about
You; and with the time my heart
Becomes more by more weak and
Breaks down, love also does start
To disappear. We can tend
To doubt that love will conk1 out
Also. When a part of body is racked with pains,
The heart is sad and depressed and is not in good
Condition for anything, except the feeling
Of the pain; and when the soul drinks so much rude
Deception, the heart is disturbed, is not being
In no condition for any proper and sane.............2

II

It is clear that the heart is connected with love
And that it perishes along with it. If eyes
Are torn from the body, it will not see again;
If your love departs from my heart, I will rise3

Nothing for you. The love and heart are then
Connected with each other by a strong bond. Above,
If the love is disturbed
By any great fear, the face
Grows pale, knees shake and eyes grow
Dim. The nature fixed the poace
And unchanged laws apropos.
It is impossible ahead
That4 spring flowers should blossom in the worn
Autumn, that wheat should ripen in the winter,
And that the gathering of grapes should take
Place in the in the spring. It is impossible further
That the man should be born not, by the sake6,
An infant, that he should grow up as soon as he is born;

III

Likewise it is impossible that the earth could
Be productive without rains. It is impossible
That should cross the sea on feet. Here also man
Weighs the gain of help in the life of possible
State against the loss. Man does not reject certain
Social life and he loves people, yet in his good
Opinion "it is better
To do kindness than to then
Receive kindness." For the law
Of state must be obeyed in
Order that one may be raw7
Saved from punishment and fire
Of punishments; wise man loves all human races,
Life, and their pleasures, yet he carefully even
Avoids becoming enslaved to them. There is nothing
That is more hateful to me than lack of culture. Then,
Except for a few, most of poets are pursuing
Glory that gives them blessing, happiness, riches;

IV

And they8 do not educate the people but they9
Corrupt them by filling their minds with some empty
Tales and harmful superstition. No man of sense
Will hate the errings, otherwise he will be
Sick10 of himself. Let him reflect how many dense
Times he offer against morality some day,
How many times of his deed11
Stand in need of pardon; then
He will be very angry
With himself. How much human
To manifest toward only
Wrondoers as kind, splendid
And fatherly spirit, not hurting them down but
Calling them back! Man must accustom himself to
Look upon death not as an evil and a real
Misfortune, but as the law of nature. Do you
Wish to be acceptable to God? Then be still
Good, to serve him is to imitate him as a nut12.

V

It is not to employ sacrifices but to
Have a righteous and upright attitude;
For the human life rests upon beneficence
And harmony. Man is a sacred and so good
Thing to man. Therefore, it is necessary to thence
Love men, even sinful ones. Moral decline to
Will end only by means of
Moral cleansing13 of human
Being of every single
Personality, and then
A cleansing that shall rekindle14
Divinity in man-dove

To overcome the animal and the beast in
Him. Therefore we are not to repay evil
To evil, but to pardon and to forget. And
If the wise man receives a blow on the little
Cheek, he will do what Cato the Roman had planned
Or did:< This is the true greatness of soul often:

VI

Love of virtue, amiability, goodness
Of heart. For whoever is not good is not great;
A man will neither be good nor else great, because
Greatness of soul is a thing unshakable, straight,
Uniform and strong from the bottom, and it draws
Something that cannot exisl in evil or faithless
Nature. Evil men may be
Terrible, turbulent, and
Destructive, but greatness
They will never really tend
To have for its buttress15
And stay is goodness truly.
We have the essential idea of the splendid
Saying in the wisdom of Solomon: "Therefore
Wisdom cannot enter a deceitful soul, or
Live in a body in debt to sin. There is more
Sanctity in the human life, and this encore
Sanctity can be showed as perfect by good deed."

VII

The happy life, therefore, is a life that is in
Harmony with its own nature, and the happy
Man is he who allows reasonto fix value
Of every condition of existence. Really,
Man must do what his nature requires him to do,

Since it is his own truth; for noman can even
Be said to be quite happy
If he were truted outside
The pale of truth. The sound, strong,
And good mind does not fear side
Of anything __ not even long
Pain and some discourtesy.
Virtue without an adversity grows weaks. For
We saw above that not even death is to be
Feared, since death is a law of nature by which soul,
Freed from the prison of the natural body,
Returns to the heavens where it came as a whole.
To humble oneself is the freedom, furthermore.

VIII

To be obedient to God, to the receive
Everything in love and without complaint, and not
To be agited even if evil springs forth
From good. For the man who orders his life a lot
Is freed from suffering; apart from death,henceforth,
For only one thing frees us from pains, from active
Humiliations, and wound
Of living: "for the precept
Of wisdom, or as we would
Say today and thus accept:
Science, philosophy." Good
Science and very profound
Philosophy will comfort you, they will cheer you;
If in earnest they gain the entrance to your mind,
Nevermore will sorrow enter there, nevermore
Anxiety, nevermore useless and unkind
Distress of the futile suffering. Furthermore,
We are responsible our own suffering too.

IX

For he who advanced toward the higher realm amnd
Lifted to higher levels drags a loosened a chain;
He is not yet free, but still is as good as free.
Wisdom makes us free. But wisdom must be so sane,
Modest and moral. I am not a wise body.
And one requires from me that I should be so grand
And equal I should be better
Than wicked. It is enough
For me if every day to lower
The number of my so tough
Vices, to blame my strongest
Mistakes. By means of moral strength and confidence,
Man is able to improve his character and
To win victory over himself from day to
Day; thus lie will be able to celebrate grand
Holiday everyday. Even though man can too
Become virtuous, it is forbidden with sense
To man to rebuke and to
Curse other men even though
Sin provokes grievous complaints,
Since the worst sin come back of blow
Understanding. The cotents
Of Socrates let us too
To understand that the understanding has been
Put into the mind of man in order that he
May reject the evil and choose the good. The true
Beauty is not found in external frippery
But is achieved by the virtuous deeds of due
Men. And the deeds of men are not to have been
Judged according to their
External appearances,
But according to intention
And purpose in them. This is

Impure thoughts or conception
Are to be included under
Term "error", and error comes only from a lack
Of understanding of the good; and when a man
Commits an error while intending to do good
To himself, he only makes harm to himself; then
Each mistake involves a contradiction so rude.

1-conk out means die. 2-the dots of suspension replace thought. 3-rise means feel in the improper sense. 4- worn means conjunctive. 6-sake means design. 7- raw is an adverb and means naively. 8-and they do not educate, they replces poets. 9-but they corrupt, they replaces poets. 1- be sick means hate. 11-deed is written at the singular because of the rhyme.. 12-nut means devotee in the improper sense. 13- cleansing means purification. 14-rekindle means stir up, awaken. 15-buttress means support.

No 40

Unexpecting meeting

Jack reminded himself to conquer
Some beautiful women by a great
Action of splendor. I was constantly
And deeply moved what must I love straight,
If New- York does not then accept me?
I rescued a charming and tender
Women who just fell
At ten steps of me;
I help demoiselle
Up and we truly
Adore each other,
She hastens to know
My soul. Moreover,
It is to follow
The phases of love that unknow to
Misis Grant just appears in her heart
For Von. Forgive me, dear charming,and
If my talks smell distress! Since I part
You my soul, I commence to withstand;
They should smell like me powder of new
Desire. Angelic
Lover who does steal
My mind, I thus peek
You and me until
In the middle
Of divinity,

We have to crumble1
For being really
Virtuous. Cover your proper breast
That I do not have to see: with such
Alike objects the souls are wounded;
And that make the guilty thoughts come much.
I am very tender to ill-bred
Temptation, and flesh on my purest
Sense makes many great
Impressions. Meanwhile
My prayers quite straight
Do not have the vile
Merit for having
Attracted this grace
Higher in standing;
According to pace
To heaven I have made no devout
Solicitation that did not have
For object you convalescence. Whence
My chest does not shut up a grave
Heart that his a rock. For me, I hence
Think that all your sighs then reach out
To the sky, and that
Nothing on-earth do
Not arrest your fat
Desires. For the true
Love that ties us to
The heavenly beauties
Does not strangle too
The intimacies
Of temporaries; our own senses
Easily can be charmed by perfect
Works that the sky made. Your reflect
Charms(human beauty is a reflect

Of divine beauty) radiated
In your equals, but it displays with ease
The marvels in you.
I feel that my heart
Reaches a taboo2,
Ardent love as art,
To the most beautiful
Pictures where God himself
Paints. My soul is full
With his joy as elf;
She told: "And your speeches vainly
Pretend to oblige me to the leave
The pleasure of being able to
Revenge me. I would like to live
Or to serve him the best of my due
Soul, but the interest of heavenly
God would not be then
Able to agree
It. Commerce even
Would bring blameworthy
Action between us,
But God knows what all
Human beings thus
Thought about our gall3.
This is an extreme sweetness to just shove4
Those words from mouth that I love. Their honey
In all my senses make a suaveness
Flow that we never tasted truly.
The bliss of pleasing you is my endless
Supreme study, my heart of your love5
Makes its peace that thence
Surpasses certain
Understandings. Whence
If I have to then

Talk about me with you,
I do not entrust
Me with sweet talks, too
A so little just
Favor does not come to make me sure
Of all that they can tell me: plant
In my soul a fixed faith of charming
Bounties that you have for me. Content
I am! Your love acts in unswerving
Tyran, it throws my mind in a unique
Trouble! It takes on my heart a frantic.......6

1-crumble means die. 2- taboo is a qualificative adjective of love and means sacred, untouchable. 3-gall means impudence. 4-shone means come out, proceed out in the improper sense. 5-my of your love makes its peace that surpasses certain understandings = my heart makes of your love its peavce that thence surpasses certain understandings. 6-the dots of suspension replace empire.

No 41

Feeling of love

I

What a charn, since I am indeed condemned as you
To satirical songs and to melodrama
For life, to listen a work of human language
In pure dialect, to be clear with brouhaha
Of this vulgary patois as pupilage
That they speak and that they write today, it is true.

II

As this phrase is neat, brusk, alert! As the mind thence
Crakles to shock of dialogue! How much malice,
And at the same time what a tenderness! In fact,
The mouth smiles and the eyes shine, glossy by amiss
Emotion. Scene of love under trees is an act
Of a sweet pity, of a pure passion that hence..............1

III

My mind that is not at all refractory to
The charms of mystery, loves too much brightness for
Getting lost in the obscurantism of due
Metaphysic or for being strayed encore
In the cloudy world of geniuses and true
Fairies, in some cloudy religions quite undue.

IV

Remind to this mind so pure while James and Vicky
Find themselves under the trees of Prospect park; then
As them, pay attention: "This is the voice of night,
This is the song of bird that invite to heaven."
With them, contemplate Venus the star of the right
Love the most beautiful pearl of nights on the sea.

V

Find out as James that the stars love each other and
Look for each other, that2 the moon takes form for kissing
The ocean, that3 the forests and rocks tend to speak,
And you will feel yourself too much condescending4
Of the world of fantasy. From the specific
Twenty century, this romantism comes to end

VI

Neither in the feelings, nor in the ideas, nor
In the expressions, you hencefort find nothing than
The vigor that animates personages
Of "one does not joke." What James and Vicky often
Loses in the romance is the extrasensories
Quite psychological that possesses them more.

VII

Far of having the religion of love, James is
Sceptic on the virtue of women and affect
To judge the loving life of a positive and
And disabused manner. He wants to show to perfect
Uncle that young women better raised up, wakened
Are quite ready to yield to a seducer with ease.

VIII

For romance,James sees only the dandy side
With all that he implies a lot of contemptuous
Skepticism and a lot of libertinahge so
Affected. If he yields at the love and thus
Decides with joy to the marriage apropos5.
This comedy seems to obey to laws as pride,

IX

This is to say to conventions, and to wonts
Of proverbs of sitting room, we thus discover
Quite close of heart. The salvation by the woman
Mixes up with salvation of marriage. After,
This is not a girlfriend but a wife that James wants.
1-the dots of suspention replace ravish. 2-that the moon
takes form for kissing, that being a relative pronoun of James
is the complement of direct object of takesthat the forests
and rock tend to speak, that a relative pronoun of James is
the complement of direct objrct of verb tend to spesk. 4-
condescending means diatant. Apropos means appropriate.

No 42

Amazing world

I

Von, the poet of incandescent Passion, wo
Is burned cruelly by its heat, carries in him
The nostalgy of a world in order, whence love
May light up in peace, whereas others assure prim
And social stability. He wants a world of
Order, but the order of love, a love quite true.

II

By this clecer reemployment, Von shows that he
Remains faithful to himself and that the ordeal
Of Brooklyn changed nothing to his so intimate
Conviction. All the people live because they still
Look for each other, and the suns will fall in straight
Dusts, if one of between them stop loving really.

III

Life and love are one and even act for Von. By
There his humanismis spared by the lower
Middle-class quality, where he had a good chance
Of getting bogged; his marriage at the cover
Of safe is part of big gravitation of dense
Stars. This is on another bridge that his fate makes shy.......1

IV

Between lies and truth, between straw and grain of things,
Between language and silence; Von attained sickness
Of talk: he envelopes, circumvent, does smother
His uncle by some discourses. Nevertheless,
Loodmillard is a mute personage, who ever
Wakes up rather than love wakes up the sayings.

V

The role of Loodmillard is a silentious role,
One of those marvelous and impossible roles
Where all are in the presence, the tone, the regard.
But the best role is justly there: in this decent
Righteousness, this exact common sense, this hard2
And direct institution of matters as whole.

VI

That permits Loodmillard of never ceding to
The illusions and lies of appearances or
Of the imagination. She said to master
Of dance, when you want not to fall, you must watch more
In front of you. When master of dance, who ever
Has the extravagance of the adults, finds too
Natural to look at the left when one is going
To right, and to right when one is going to left.
Loodmillard knew how to keep the privilege
To go right to the matters and to even heft3
Them. This real look is never the lack of knowledge
Of simple little goose as they are pretending.

VII

Her innocence is not defenseless, it very
Nearly happened. She give to it the masterful
Proof when she must undergo the pressing assaults
Of seducers. A subtle smile passed on the full
Of her lips, and outlined as a slight shade of vaults3
The both dimples of her cheeks. The glance of a kindly
Lover only sees such smiles, for we feel it more
Than we do not see them. This smile went until soul,
And swallowed it as a temperance; but by strange
Bizarreness, the remind of this moment of sole
Delights links itself in my mind as an exchange.
Do you pretend that all the women are encore 5

VIII

And all husbands are deceived? I pretend nothing,
And I know nothing about it. I pretend, when
I am going to the street, not to put myself
Under the wheels of cars; when I dine, not to then
Eat the whiting; when I am thirsty as an elf,
Not to drink in a broken glass; when I am seeing
A woman, not to marry her; and often
I am not sure not to be either crushed or chocked,
Or breach-tooth. Ah! Coquette woman! This is again
Around fire that you turn as a dazzled and joked
Butterfly. Do not talk about it, since you then
Forgiveness and you come along with again.

IX

Do not spoil a precious moment! My Loodmillard,
How beautiful you are, what bliss reposes in you!
By what oaths, by what treasures may I pay your sweet
Kisses? Ah! The life would not be enough. And too,

Come on my heart; let yours feel it; normally beat,
And let this nice sky carries them to Godas art.

X

Lookat how this night is pure! How this wind heaves on
Your shoulder this avaricious gaze that hence
Surrounds them! Pay attention, this is the sweet voice
Of the night; this is the song of the bird that thence
Invite to the happiness. Behind this raised choice6
Rock, no single look can discover us whereon.
All sleep except those who love each other. Ask to
Forests and rocks what they would tell if they could say?
They have love in their hearts and cannot express it.
I love you, this is what I know, you have no way;
This is what this flower tells you, she who did meet
In bowels of earth the sugars that must feed it too.
1-the dots of suspension replace light. 2-hard means firm,
solid. 3-heft means estimate. 4-vaults means jumps. 5-the
dots of suspension replace false. 6- choice means rare.

No 43

My beloved Odette

I

You are the comfort of my soul
In the season of sorrow. For
Let me go into your life, you
Must have the courage to therefore
Listen your conscience; this is true
Echo of my voice in your whole
Heart, that1 directs you to authentic
Love and that2 tells you when you are
Selling yoiurself short. The voice that
Sings your name is sweeter so far
Than stars who sleep tenderly threat3,
Than song of Witney so lyric.

II

O love, fly back to your native
Land; you thus broke free from cage;
And your wings are earnest to flight.
At times you must suppress your sage
Conscience, seeing it as the right
Enemy of freedom and active
Love. But you have the courage to
Follow it. You and I will have
Life and have it abundantly.
You are the pure liquor, my brave

Heart is the cup. Without your honey
Liquor, what is use of this due.........4?

III

Listen to the call of my heart,
How it wails with the pain of break.
The call of my heart comes from fire,
What is use of my life without this wake
Fire? It is fire of love that prior
Brings music to my heart as art.

IV

It is ironic that you find
The freedom and love you desire
In the place you less expect in true
Obedience of the higher
Law of the nature. And if you
Desire love, you must have the kind
Courage to take a deep look into
The motives of your heart, a deep
Look at the meaning of sex. Too,
The call is the ferment that lets slip
The taste to the liquor of Jew.
The call of my heart soothes pain of few 5

V

Do not be happy with promises
Of other men, I am the true
Tabernacle of happiness; let
The light of your heart guide you
To my houser. Let light of your wet
Heart show that we are one. with ease,
My soul tends to fly away when

Your bush calls my name so sweetly.
I am the light, you are the moon.
Do not rise without me. Truly,
If you retreat from the jejune
Challenge of looking at your heart, then
If you act as if there is no
Fault in you that needs correction,
You deceive yourself. You always
Make frustration in projection
Of your good will not to mix rays
Of lust with love; you are a beau.
1-that directs you, that being a relative pronoun of voice
is the subject of verb directs. 2-and that tells you, that
being a relative pronoun of voice is the subject of verb tell.
3-thereat means at that place. 4-the dots of suspension
replace cup.. 5-the dots of suspension replce lost love

No 44

Adultery

I

You who get up and leave with the heart
Full of the felicities of night,
With the tranquil spirit, with the smart
Mind, are going to ruminate1 aright
On your happiness as those who chew again
After diner the taste of richer
Truffles that they digest so often
Or that they happily mull over.

II

Remind the day we walked farther
Around a little lake where freckles
Of water made a green on tender
Waves. And with all my colored speckles,
I tell you: "I am wrong, and so wrong
I am. I am glad and sad to
Listen your reproaches quite long."
Odette! My dear, do not boohoo2!"

III

Oh! you said in hanging yourself on
My shoulder. You overthrow your neck
That swelled up with sigh and tears upon

My mistake, with an overlong peck3
Of shudder, and hiding your nice face.
When you are recovered from this load,
When after having shaken the pace
Of my cheating, you came back to abode,

IV

Where you have to find a true husband
Who adores you, after his first fault,
After this first adultery quite planned,
After this first fall as an assault.
Odette! I am forgiven by
You. You have never eyes so open,
So red, either of such a depth. Nigh,
Something subtle extretched on your person..............4

V

You always told: "I have a lover!
A lover who finds pleasure in this
Idea as in this one of another
Puberty that would have amiss
Happened quickly. You went finally
To possess those pleasures of love, and
This ferver of the delight whose he
Specifictly dispairs and does strand5;

VI

A lover who enters into something
Wonderful, where everything would be
Passion, ecstasy, ranting and raving6.
Thus, from this first fault, from this first wee
Fall, you do the grandiosity,
You sing the ode of licentiousness,

Its pleasure-seeking, its poetry,
And its normal voluptuousness."

VII

I had the mania to chatter
In the sitting room, I did not do
It in that day. You had short-temper;
If your eyes could; they would squeeze me through
By the wall. At last, you started
Your toilette of night, then you even
Took a book and continued your stead8
Reading as if reading cheered you then.

VIII

Remember when I already lied
Down in the bed, I called you and told:
"Come, Odette! It is time to decide
For slleping. "you answered me with a cold
Voice: "Yes, I come." And then you never
Come. I put on my dressing gown, then
I passed my arm around your nicer
Waist and brought until back of garden..

IX

That was under arbor, on the same
Bench where formerly I admired you
So lovely during the nights of maim
Summer! I knew to tell you some true
And sweet words that made tell one day:
"The love is a sacred authencity
Coming from God, I will never betray
It; I promise you to remain trusty9."

X

You remember that I turned this same
Sacred wish to you, and now I made
Mistake that makes our sacred love lame.
How many times I asked you the shade
Of forgiveness, and to thence accept
My apology. Remind encore
One more time that the coldness of wept
Night made us embrace each other more,

XI

The sighs of your lips seemed stronger,
Your eyes that glimpsed tended to appear
Wide-open, in the middle of stranger
Silence there were certain words quite fair
Coming out lowly, that nicely
Jumped on my heart with a christallyne
Sonority and that tenderly
Reflected in doubled vibriations so keen.

1-ruminate meanshave one'smind 2-boohoo means cry,
weep. 3-peck means blow. 4-the dots of suspension replace
transform it. 5-strand means twist.6-rating and raving is
an expression that means delirium. 7-grandiosity menas
glorification. 8-stead means quiet. 9-trusty means faithful

No 45

Pleasure-seeking

I

Do you know in the world a language more
Expressive? Have you never seen encore
A lascivious paint?
Listen at the instant:
Odette at this era,
Vicky never looked, ah,
Nice, she had this indefinissable
Beauty that then results from the admissible
Joy, from the excitement1,
From the accomplishment,
And that is normally
The great harmony
Of amorous nature or of outlook
With the circumstances, sometimes her snook2.

II

Her passion, her grief, the experience
And her illusions always young, intense
As the manure, the rain,
Winds and sun do to fain
Flowers, by graduation,
Grew her in elation,
And she radiated in plenitude
Of her nature. Her eyelids seemed trim, a prude

For her long loving looks
Where gets lost in tyro looks,
Whereas a strong breeze hence
Spead her thin nostril, thence
It raised fleshly corner
Of her lips and waist; further,
Something subtle that went in you got free
From draperies of her dress, from her gradely..........4

III

Until the beauty of this woman had
Consisted in her grace, in her glad
Outward form, in her dresses,
In the way she expresses
In the she smiles, she walks,
In the way she thus talks
And welcomes the lovers. And finally,
She comes to be shown very clearly
To you, and you can tell
If theso nonpareil
Adultery has not
Improved herlook a lot.
She cries out: "Take me woith you! I beg you!
Take me away as star will guide us too."

III

She hastens on his lips, as for catching
The unexpected consent, exhaling
Herself in a kiss. Is there
In this woman unfair
And adulterous who
Used to going to
Church, something of the faith of repentant

Magdalena? No, this is always servant
Or passionate woman
Who looks for the omen5
Illusions, who looks for
Them in the places more
Sainted, and more august. One day sickness
Pushed her to believed to be in thoughtless 6

IV

She asked for prayer; as much as they made
In her bed room the plans for the parade
Service, her maid put on
The table a so shone
Bible for the preacher,
And a bsattle of the water.
Vicky felt something so strong passing
On her, that released her from her hulking
Pains, from all perception,
And from all conception.
Her lightened flesh did not
Weighed anymore, not a lot;
Another life started,
It seemed to her ahead
That her being that went up to God were
Disappearing itself in love ever,

V

As a lighted encense dissipating
Itself in steam. In what manner of speaking
Do they pay to humbler
God with the words that were
Addressed to lovers in
Effusions of certain

Adultery? Without doubt, they let out
Of the color of church, they just point out
Of telling that a woman
So vaporous, often
Romanesque, does not do,
Even in the statue
Of religion, things as all devotees.
There is no local color that excuses.......7

VI

Voluptuous one day and religious
Tomorrow, no wife even in previous8
Regions, under
The sky of the Denver
Or New-York, does not whine
To God the cheating of fine
Kisses that she gave to the lover. Ah!
If in the freshness of her beauty, aah,
Before stains of wedlock
And desillusions of shock
Adultery, she could
Place her life on some good
And great heart quite solid, then the virtue,
Tenderness, pleasure-seeking, duty too
Confoundind themselves; never she would be
Descended from a high felicity.

VII

In seeing John on stage, she had envy
To run in his arms for taking easy
Refuge in her strength, even
In flesh and blood, to then
Exclaim: "Take me with you!
Take me away as true

Man! Let us leave! All my zeals are to you!"
Tim stepped behind her, leaning on the due.........9
Against the bulkhead; whence
From time to other, she thence
Felt shivering under
Warm breath from his ruder
Nostrils descending in the hair. They now
Talked to us about stains of wedlock; how
They are goingto show us adultery
Is in her nameless charms in all her poetry.

VIII

Vicky tells that they should modify cogent
Expressions and tells:the disappointement
Of marriage and stains
Of cheating. Quite often,
When you get married, instead
Of happiness without spread
Clouds that the men promised, we only met
The hard sacrifices and the regret,
Bitterness. Almost,
The words after the most
Kisses hurled themselves. Whence
We met sorrows of dense
Forebodings, the inquietudes for
Talking to each other; but now encore
All are just forgotten,
We faced each other, then
With smiles of pleasure seeking
And of title or naming
Of tenderness.   The warm flat8,with its careful
Carpet, its frisky ornaments, its restful
Light, seemed quites comfortable for any
Intimacy of passion or frenzy..............10

IX

Vicky laughed over a vribrant laughter
And libertine, when the froth of better
Wine of Champagne jutted
Over the light-footed10
Glass on the rings nof her
Fingers. They were ever
So completely lost in the possession of
Themselves, that they felt like being above
In their particular
Houses so spectacular,
And having to enjoy
Until death as a boy,
As two admirable
Young spouses so able.
John savors for first time, in exercise
Of love, the unspeakable and unwise
Delicateness of the so feminine
Gentility or elegance quite routine.

X

John has never met this grace of language,
This reserve of garment, this carriage
Of drowsy dove. He then
Admired the joy of the open
Exaltation of her soul
And laces of her sole
She had words that inflames him with kisses
That took him away. When had she, with ease,
Those nice kisses almost
Immaterial, most
Deep, dissimilated?
Oh! I comprehended

Quite the distate that her husband who still wanted
To hug her at her return; I concluded
Wonderfully that when the rendez-vous
Of this species normally tookplace, too,

XI

Vicky felt with horror, the night, against
Her flesh, this adulterated and minced
Man who slept. Out of self,
She then poison herself.
She poisoned herself, why?
Ah! This is a little sly
Thing, the death, did she normally think;
I am going to fall asleep or sink11
And all will be finished.
Then without an anguished
Remorses, without a wish,
Without any forewish
To repent on the suicide that get
Achieved, she is gpoing to receive yet
The last sacraments
Of the dying gents12,
In her thought, now she is
Going to obscurities?
Why, when there is no tear, not a sigh
On her crime of disbelief, on her wry
Suicide, on her adulteries? After
This cause, this one of prayer will enter.

XII

Those are the sainted and sacred words for
All. Those are withthose words that we therefore
Put our ancestors to
Sleep, our fathers, and too
Our fellows. And those are
With them that our bizarre
Children will put us to sleep. When we then
Want to reproduce them, we must even
Do it accurately.
We do not have to only
Connect them with so lewd
Form on past-life quite crude.
The preacher got up for taking holy
Cup13; she stretched neck as someone who is really
Thirsty; she finally
Pressed her lips on the body
Of man-God, and she put
From all her dying chute
Or force in it the greatest kiss of love
That she had never given. For above
All, she read psalms. After,
She puts her right finger
In the holy oil and
Started onctions that tend
To really covet all voluptuous
Sumptuosities, first on the eyes, thus
On the nostrils, tasty
Of warm land-air quite breezy
And of loving odor,
Then bush that were ever
Open for the lies, that bemoaned her pride
And solved in luxury in other side;
Then on the hands that found

Pleasure in nice profound
And suave approavches
Formerly when, with ease,
She ran to the satisfying of her
Desire that now would not go well. Further
Do you want to refresh
Your eyes on moist and fresh
Jasmine? Do you want to feel
Feel your body fading too
As in a wave in the sweet flesh of breaded
Women, I took pleasure to ask her?

1-Excitement means enthusiasm. 2-snook meansridicule expression. The dots of suspension replace instep. 5-omem used as a qualificative adjective of illusions. 6-the dots of suspension replaceagency. 7-the dots of suspension replace mixture. 8-previous means other in the improper sense. 9-the dots of suspension replace shulder. 10-flat means apartment. 11-the dots of suspension replace of desire. Light-footed means light. 12-sink means die. 13-cup means holy cup means sacraments.

No 46

Charming woman

I

O Odette! This lily of chastity,
Sad, the dreamer of forehead, but full of heart
And dignity, of virtue, but pure as
A ray that the morning as a sweet heart
Sees arising. Your name is enough as
Making your known in the community.

II

Forgive me, sublime woman, if my words
Smell the distress! Since in good lover
I suffer, it should therefore smell as me
Powder of desire. Celestial courter
Who brought my heart and my audacity.
I see you in the breast of women-birds.............!1

III

Most cruel I can name: tiger,
Lions and bears, sneaks, strange monsters; you laugh
At me by killing me and I die for
Loving. Thus the minced games tempt our minds, and
Reserve for a day our brave love to more
Let fly the little kisses that may tend
To wish since we will be spouses, no gaff.

IV

If in the middle the deaths, you envy
To wake me up, you must put down other
Life. My soul calls the skies with a saintful
Passion, put instead of my manner
Of speaking your language of pitiful
Woman that I am only a heavenly...........2
The celestial mysteries appeared to
You for seeing the beautiful secrets amnd
The paints that we inspire, whether a dream
Gave you an image to morning quite bland,
Whether in swoon the mimnd did its extreme
Trips; that keeps you in a dream quite undue.

VI

You prove a visible sympathy for
The humbles, for the beauties of nature
If I do not abuse myself to read
Your heart, you will command me to answer
To your desire. Tell me again or proceed
Out what makes you judge on my desire new.

VII

Learn one more time what hope I must take about it;
A so diamond-bright speech that is not possible
To much understand. You are now quiet,
This is quite well. Let us speak a little
But why do we want us to parry yet
The name our parents? This is exquisite.

VIII

Because those are them who raise us. And then nobles
Of the heart is much worthier than the other3.
The virtue is above the nobless. I really
Am not among them that principle or order
Specifictly wounds. In fact, to the contrary,
That flatters me and smiles me nevertheless.

IX

When we have talents, when we have the mind,
When we are young and beautiful, when
The nature-mother gave us this feature,
This air, this expression, this stature, then
This foot, this leg, this arm, this nice figure,
Whose the heat illumines a fight quite kind.

X

You see it, good I am! I always appear
Risible. You forgive me easily,
A slip quite calamitous and so light.
This fault is not bigas secondary
Planet8.why do you excuse yourself? Right,
You have quite well told. My dear, you are fair!

XI

You agree that I have much brain! This is not
The vanity of my part, I swear you,
Each one feels his weight and knows his limit.
You will have honor of winning the true
Prize when we are husband and wife. My fit
Angel, star of universe, you're my spot!

XII

You come to inspire me many unequal
Verses. As the glace to sun, I thus feel
Melt my soul. The heat of the hell do
Not equal my heat. This is you who still
Paint the love! What the most expressive, too
The noblest at same time, the most primal!

XIII

You, my beautiful flower blue and red,
A little bachelor's button, who thus
Listen me, the inclined forehead, without
Telling a word! See your tint of lustrous
Rose, your resplendent face many stout
Spirit repose. Odette, you smile instead!

XIV

You have the talent of pleasing. You speak
Of gold. In your honor and glory
This beautiful speech must figure in verse.
Doubtlessly, it might the eulogy
To my person quite very so diverse.
If I recall it, I will write it, pick........5

XV

You will see how to court the beautiful
Women, hpow to go about subduing
The rebels. I dare to adore you. Without
The pity of my heart for then seeng
The tears? Be fair, may I resist to your doubt
Or to your charm and to your wonderful 6

XVI

You agree that my style is so tender
And so generous. I knew to find
The good way in your heart. For I listen
Nothing, nothing if not the oath quite kind,
Nothing if not the promise to often
Love me from an equal tenderness ever
1-the dots of suspension replce or divinity. 2-the dots of
suspension replace voice. 3- the dots of suspension replace
nobles. 4-secondary planet means moon. 5- the dots of
suspension replace it. 6-the dots of suspension replace shape

No 47

Listen carefully

I

An imperceptible smile passes on the nook
Of lips of a woman, and draws as a fine look
The both dimples of your cheeks. The eyes of a beau
Uniquely perceives such a smile quite apropos.
This is the better that you wrote me, o mister!
Those are the wind and rain moaning on this flyer.

II

No, my Odette, those are the joy and the love; and
Those are bliss and desire as you are in demand.
O my lass, beautiful you are; and then what grace
Rests in you! By what sworn statement or by what pace,
By what treasure may I pay your sweet kisses? Ah!
The life is not enough, as this one in Utah.

III

Come on my heart, and yours feels it beat; and the sky
Carries them to God! See how this night is so shy
And pure! Listen carefully:" this is the sweet voice
Of the night and the warble of birds that rejoice
Us. Behind this big tree, no glance can discover
Us. All are calm, expect the two tender lover.

IV

My dear, I have under my arm the deceitful
Demon that the hell never vomits. Beautiful
Is the river that speaks to me; it appears this one
Of angel, and it opens to me the alone
Route of the sky. But the morals are the highest
Perfection of human existence and the best
Ultimate aim of all methods. When we taste thus
The morals in our relation so precious.
Then we feel the real happiness because the laws
Of moral are not fictional, this is my cause.

V

The word of the tears pleases me as the star, and
I do not know the reason. A pleasant and grand
Sky gives the energy of tearing. And you,
It just gives you the envy og singing the dew.
Me, envy of loving you, of living for you!
Odette, do you know to whom you in a few
Word, and what is the man who dares to embrace you?

No 48

Illusion

I

We are under illusion, we are living then
As if the love is our factual self. Even
It is our property, we suppose to keep it
In good sanity. My thought is very licit.
Tell me the name of star that naturally
Illumines your heart and your spirit quite lively.

II

Eh well! This Venus, the star of love, the most
Shining, pearl of ocean, of nights! It is our host.
There is one the chastest, quite worthy of respect;
You will learn to love it one day, when you connect
In the small farms, and you will have many poors
With you; aedmire them while I guard my smile; keep yours.
This is Ceres, goddess of bread. I really know
That you have a tender heart, and you are my beau.

III

O my nice lass! I guess the bottom of your heart,
You do the charity. You always see apart
The cosmic goodness; and me too, but in yoiur eyes.
Life is in the love, since ocean that horrifies
Under the pale kisses of Diana until

Beetle that goes to sleep jealous in its immobile
Flower-bed. Ask to the forests and to the rocks
What they would tell if they gave voice. They have the shocks
Of love in the heart and they cannot express it.
I love you! Just what I know; this what this neat1
Flower will tell you; this flower that removes out
The impure passions that can tarnish your right route.

IV

My darling! Our first interest and our first duty
Are to enlighten ourselves on this just study,
Where all behaviors depend on. Whatever
Be the content of your conceptionon better
Life, it is necessary to go behind it
If we wish to predicate existenceof neat2
Union. I should have a logical wish of putting
An end to this sophisticated mode of charming
Discourse, by a strict meaning of conception
Of life. I did not teach by my own perception
That the illusion is arising from our great
Confounding a logical with a real predicate.

V

Let us not misuse the human life in the vain
Pursuit of material enjoyment or gain.
The human existence is meant for advancing
On the path of liberation that is having
Been call freedom from entanglement. And we are
All entangled. Our acceptance of this bizarre
Extravagance and sophisticated objects3
Mean that we are already entangled. The sects
Are so confused today. We should not mentally
Grow in the process of entanglement, my glee!

VI

What entanglement I am talking about. Then
The life supposes to be really uncertain.
The function of a man is an activity
Of soul in accordance with the reason; surely,
Not independent of reason. You have to flee
Those poisonous pleasures: glory and luxury.

VII

What! I never arrive to understand. Behold,
Who does not the luxury! You make me cold.
We do not require great education of mind
To understand that on-earth is no real and kind,
Lasting assurance; that our pleasures are only
Vanity; that our evils are infinite. See,
You have two things to lose:the true and the good;
Two things to stake: your reason and your attitude4;
Your knowledge and your happiness; your quality
Has two things to the shun:mistake and misery.
I shake with fear and with joy; for I just opened
You the bottom of my heart. I am round the bend.

VIII

The sky was very clear and breeze was so gracious
When the father in his moodcame to us and said thus:
"What argument I have heard between you, children!
The birth in a well-to-do family often
Solves the problem of having to find sufficient
Food from the beginning of life, a subsequent
Comparative and more so confortable way
Of life can be led. In any which workday,
One has good chance to make progress in moral
Realization or moral conduct. Normal

Sons of a wealthy are misguided by the sense
Of enjoyment, and they forget good chance quite dense
That they have for moral enlightment. you are meant
To solve money questions of life so important
By balancing on a tottering platform; and
You are also meant to solvethe ultimate grand
Problems of life that arise due to the laws
Of the nature. Civilization will applause
By itself, will be static unless there will be
A moral move in the flow of reality."
1-neat means wonderful. 2-neat means true. 3-objects means
stuffs. Attitude means will in the improper sense.

No 49

Little rose

I

Stream intarissable, why to haggle your neat
Water to our lips? When all our thirst quite concrete
Is not enough to dry you up and that your flow
Juts out always fresh for each tended lip. Oh!
I now understand that all the drops of this wide
Well-spring are equivalent, that the least satisfied
Our transports and revealed us the plenitude and
The universality of God who is grand.

II

O beautiful Odette! I caress you under
The leaves! Never enough shade then tends to cover
Your splendor, and the shade of moonon your forehead
Appears always more somber on your flower-bed!

III

O flower of the sun! O little rose! I see
You tepid and perfumed, full of leaves and lily
Flowers! In the sublime garden of your heart shines
Our room of the inn. The suave air brings the mines
Of scent rising in the flowers of oranges,
Even the mandarins embalms all the gypsies.

IV

This is a nice place of the freshness where the charm
Of sleeping is so great that it seems quite no harm
And unknowm. And there, delicious food thus attend
When we are hungry. This is a place in demand.

V

My soul at last fills itself with lyrism; my
Loneness disturbed and exhausted me trough the shy
Nights. With you, through the nights I spoke, as if you are
A poetess. You even know accords so rare;

VI

Each natural effect became for us as nice
Language where we were able to read its precise
Cause; you learn me to discern insects by their flies,
Birds by their songs, by their steps on sands. Beauty of skies.

VII

I long for all with delice, in vain did you try
To tire our transports; each of our thoughts were a high
Verve; I feel hard for us a singular sourness.
We used our splendid youths; let us wait the flawless
Expectation, and the path that never led it further
Seem enough interminable where we lumber
At full steps, biting the river of hedges that
Flilled our mouths of a taste of honey and of flat
And exquisite bitterness. Tonight, let thence
To laud the prelude of our wedding by a dance.

VIII

Do not believe that our bliss will be therefore made
With the help of money; my heart quite unafraid
Has no attachment on-earth, just only for you.
My happiness is made with the help of your clue.
I love you, Odette! Mortal start of my soul, joy
Of heart! This is you I sing in an air so coy.

IX

Joy of my flesh, tender as the herb, so bonny
As the flowers of hedges! And when we will be
Husband and wife, we will be happy. From this time,
This will be in you that my mouth very sublime
Will get prolongated; I report on you all
My hope the most fructuous. This is my nice call.

X

Odette, I have now the heart sad. We see the rivers, we
See many branches; we cannot naturally
See the future, only the present. I see what
The instant brings, and we do not know what the pat
Tomorrow carries. We are so open to doubt
Because our unique is only to hang out.

XI

I only know that one advances by driving
behind self the past. The story was describing
that the wife of Lot, for having wanted to look
behind, turned in statue of salt. Raise again shook
of your head, and then permit at last that your heart
fills not with vanity, but with love; and be smart.

XII

Yes, permit again that all caresses of air,
The raysof sun, and all invitations of fair
Happiness, attain your niceheart and fill your mind
With wisdom and with all things that are very kind.

XIII

How I long for you, little rose! Whence incline through
Yourhands, through you're the nice branches of Crestview
Trees at fruits. I listen a suave song through your
Heart, a nice song that I invent at my guise more
Words that strengthen my heart; a song I determine
Your name, your smile! This is time to come back Brooklyn.

No 50

Rapturous triumph

I

Lood, at Brooklyn, last night I came to chaperon1
The rapturous triumph of great Toni Braxton.
Indeed, you would have shared as me the natural
Pride and joy, if you could see again this normal
Grace and this personified poetry. And you
Would have smiled with satisfaction to see this true
Rain of crowns and of bouquets that have constantly
Abounded the podium. This was a dainty
House of applauses, without exaggeration.
The pretty time that she took with moderation
For picking them up has been for the spectators
A prolongation of pleasure and of fervors.

II

How many divine smiles, ineffable kisses,
Sweet thanks of heart, expressed by of charming nudges2,
Has not she sent back to them by her divine
Hand while she was graciously occupied, fine
Flower among the flowers, to collect bouquets
That did stop flowing on her from all lengthaways
Of boxes, without except the imperial
Box! She was covered by a soft material.
If I was painter, what joy! What an exhibit!
The enthusiasm at its mix! From the pit

207

Until curve, in all galleries, in all lodges,
All bushes smiled at rapture, all phisionomies
Were sparkled, all hands applauds. Women and men,
Young and old, enthusiasm has all taken.
All deaths got out of their sepulchers. Those were wit3,
Cheers, dampings, until there were no atome of grit4
In the cracks of the floor of the calling that has not
Taken its flyon the wings of fire of this fat
And irresistible enthusiasm, and
That has not contributed to form as a grand
And dense cloud of encense whose the large playroom
Was surrounded; there was no place for the mushroom.

IV

Taken with such an admiration for Toni,
I feel like engendering in me a folly
Quite forceful to see close to me this wonderful
Woman. She has a shape quite very beautiful.
I fall in love. Of course, she has a shape so trimful.
Normally, do you think that I am more careful
To accents of a nice voice than the pirouette
Of a beautiful leg. Hey, she is my shouette5.

V

For the grace of her nice legs she joins all graces
Of heart and of spirit. She moves me as a breeze.
She shows me her charming legs for troubling my mind,
For rousing my sense, for winning my heart so kind.
In order that the man finds a nice souvenir
Of skies and keep it in his memory so dear.
1-chaperon means attend in the improper sense. 2-nudges
means gesture. 3- wit means screams. 4-grit means
dusts. 5-my shouette means my girl, my lover.

No 51

I

The nice collections of our wonderful passed years
With so much tranquility left for us the cheers
And thousand charming impreesions that we long for
Recalling endlessly in our epoch encore.
I have a guide so fidele on which I may be sure,
This is the chain of my feelings that marked the pure
Succession of my being, and by them this one
Of events that have been cause or effect, I run.

II

I easily forget my hutrts, but I cannot
Forget my mistakes, and I forget again a lot
Of nice sentiments. I can make the omissions
On the facts, the misses of dates, the tranpositions;
But I cannot just deceive on what I did feel,
Neither on what my feelings had me made as real.
Objects of my shrifts is to let know my inside
In the touching situations of your life-side.

III

This is story of my soul that I promitted,
And for writing it I do not need other read
Memories. It is enough to enter inside

Me as I did at this moment, this is my pride.
I let me shroud in the night of times, what I have
To say; I am obliged to talk despite me; grave
I was. I was therefore reduced me and to lie,
To try to give the change, to degrade myself by
The things for which I am not born. I normally
Dodged all that is good in the community.

IV

At the instant of this long lecture, you plan
For another mode; I devine another man.
Those are the singularities of your bitter
Hint1 that have to betold, as soon you deliver
It on a paper, it abandons you; as soon
As you write a thing, you don't remind it, my boon!

 V

My dynamism showed itself to the deepness
Of my thoughts with the most impossible fastness.
All my great passions were smotheredby excitement
Of the truth, of the freedom, of the sentiment
Of virtue; and what there is the most amazing
Is that this effervescence remained so living
In my heart for more several years, at a level
Perhaps it has not been in another mortal2.

VI

Sincere with myself, too proud inside for wanting
To give the lie on my principles by my spring
Works. I dispense myself tpo examine the true
Destination of my children and my so due
Link with their mother on the laws of the nature,
These ones of the religion pure and unending

As its author that the man spoiled in pretending
To purify it according to their profits,
To their lords of the earth, according to their wits.

VI

If I was one of those women ill-born, stone-deaf
To the sweet voice of the nature, inside of them no leaf
Of true feeling of justice, of humanity
Never sprouted; this hardness of heart would be easy.
This warmth of heart, this tenderness very lively,
This facility to form certain bloodthirsty
Attachments when it is necessary to break
Them, this good- will innate for my fellows unfake,
This love of the great, of the true, of the fine,
This horror of evil-doings in all the line,

VII

This possibility of pacifying crimes,
This impossibility of hating the times
Of war and of bothering this lively and sweet
Emotion that I feel at the aspect of neat
Lines that are virtuous, generous: do all things
Accord themselves in the same soul with wrongdoings
That truly make the rights and the duties trample
Down without a so tender heart, without scruple?

VIII

Oh, no! I loudly tell, this is impossible.
But it is true only in religious apostle3.
My soul exalted by sublime contemplations
Rises through cosmos, and I see my generations
Following these ones of their evils, of their crimes,
Of their errors in judgment in the blind routine sometimes.

Let them find me ridiculous, impertinent;
Oh! whatever they say! I must be cognizant
Of enduring the ridiculous and the fat blame,
Provided that they be not merited as chame.

IX

The most striking and numerous observations
That I gathered were above all altercations;
And by their physical principles, they appeared
Prosper to me to provide with a perservered
Exterior diet that is varied according
To the events and were able to be putting
Or maintaining the soul in the state the most censed
And favorable to the reason the most sensed.

X

Indeed, how many deviations would save
To the reason; how many vices I would shave4
To grow if I was able to force animal
Economy to favorize the principal
And moral order that it disturbs so often.
In my discipline, I have to remain certain.
Hint means memory. 2-mortal means person, human beibg. 3-apostle
is written at the singular because of rhyme. 5-shave means remove.

No 52

I

Friend of peace! I would have besides feared domestic
Storms, and I would too sincerely my so chic
Witzer for exposing him to woe for seeing
Me going to the other feelings more living.
The collections of diverse times of my life brought
Me to meditate on the point where my nice thought
Arrives, and I see me yet on the true decline
Of the age, still in prey of efficacious spine,
And thinking of touching the end of my career,
Without tasting in its plenitude almost mere,

II

None of pleasureswhose your heart was very greedy
Without having given wings to lively fancy
That I feel about it in reserve, without having
Touched this thrilling charm that you feel in your being
So stout, failure of object, it remains compressed
Without being affirmed than by my sighs so pressed.
How it is that with a soul naturally quite
Expensive I cannot find until now a right
Friend who is completely to me, a true friend; I
Who feel so well-formed for having it; you can sigh.

III

What it is that with senses so combustible,
With a heart quite kneaded by an invincible
Passion, I do not feel really burned by its flame
For an object quite well-determined. What a shame!

IV

Devoured by the need of loving, without being
Ever able to please it, I see me reaching
The doors of golden-ager, and dying without
Living the rest of my life with a love so stout.
These reflexions so sad, but heart-moving, make me
Fold back on myself with regret. It really
Seems to me that the destiny owes me something
That he has not given to me; this is touching.

VI

I make these reflexions in the most beautiful
Season of year, to month June, under flawless
Tickets so fresh, to the warbling of nightingale,
To the purling of river as a fairy-tale.

VII

All complete to dive me again in a softness
Too alluring for which I am born, o distress!
The wild feeling of my inner price makes me shed
Into tears that you love to let glide on my bed.

VIII

What ie the use of making me rise with certain
Exquisite faculties for leaving them again
Until the end without use. You are not enough
To explain my bewilderment quite very tough.

IX

Animals have no power to understand what
Is the nature and their relationship so pat
With it. Their only interests are eating, sleeping,
Mating, and fighting, and defendind and neighing.
If I am only concerned with these things, and then
What am I ? I am animal, this is certain.

X

The system is to understand the moral and
Material laws of nature and has to stand
Or to remain in relationship with them.
The laws of the nature are as a diadem.

XI

This the duty of the human beings, and
If this duty is ignored in human demand
Or the human society, and then it is
Animal community. This point makes me freeze.

No 53

Protector of children

I

Today the father and mother are not really
Protectors of the children. Husband and lady1
Of the house take care their children, this is their nice
Duty. But they are not ultimate and precise
Protectors. Although it is totally ever
Consider a fact that the father and mother
Are the protectors of children, at this time
It is not a fact. Television at the prime
Internet are the unique educators
Of most children. Parents are only helpers.

II

The immorality is for those who lead
A bad line of behavior, it is indeed
For those who invented atomic weapons, and
For those who wages the wars. They have brain quite grand,
But the atomic weapon has been misused. Then
They created something that is dreadful again,
They have to create something else that will insure
That man will no longer has to die, it is sure.
What is the use of creating something so that
Millions of people will die? Thus I ask for what?

216

III

What have the scientists done? They have to invent
Something so that there will be no disease or ailment,
To invent something so that man will not die encore,
To invent something so that there will be no more
Old age. Then they will create something not too long.
Some say atomic weapons make my country strong.
So a honest man is the one who does not steal
Any body; where the vices at last not
So scandalous either so visible a lot.

IV

I know enough that a good man is a honest
Man; but it is pleasant of opining at least
That all honest man is not a good man. Those are
Acts and comportment that reveal the man so far.
A good man is the one who is neither a true
Saint nor devout, who is confined to have virtue.
The spirit of mean rancor and of jealousy
Prevails in some leader that interest of glory,
Of the religion, of their stated, and their interes
Quite personal and domestic as their finest.

V

How much art for entering into the nature!
How much times, attention, constant work and ruler
For dancing with the same freedom and the same grace
That one knows how to behave; for singing on pace
As one speaks; for speaking and expressing as one
Thinks; to throw so much energy, of verve, of tone
And of persuasion in a prepared discourse
That the wide public disapproved with all their force.

VI

The honest man holds the middle between clever
Man and good man, although in a matchless measure.
Distance that gains between honest man and clever
Man grows weak is on the point of waning further.
The clever man is the one who hides his passions,
Who hears his interests, who feigns to have compassions,
Who sacrifices so many things, who knows how
To acquire wealth and how to conserve it now.
1-lady of the house means wife.

I

O Son! Start a new and real life, stop transferring
It in the dream; know to see it in the fitting
Reality. And if it is not real, then make
It quite so alive; we cannoit live in the fake.

II

O Vicky! You see that all that are young are tender;
And how many seeds do not envelop further
Themselves to the bud! But all that protect at first
The tender bud constrain it soon as the face-first
Germination produces, no growing is true,
Only in making burst there sprouts quite very due.

III

O Son! This is at this age where soul and flesh are
The most disposed to the love, the most on the jar
Of loving; where the clasping is the most intense,
The authority is the most sharp and immense,
And the most instructive; the voluptuousness
Is at the greatest price. This is at this flawless
Age that the soul and the body equally find
The most strength to fight desire of love so unkind.

IV

Vicky! What you called, I called with you:tentations,
Those are them I rue. If I have compensations,
This is not to have ceded at someone; only
This is to have just resisted at so many
Others, after which I run; when they were less charming
And had less profit for my thought quite consisting.
I rue for having saddened my youth, for having
Preferred imaginary than real, my darling.

V

I have often permitted to my personal
Reason to put an end to the unnatural
Transport of craziness. Vicky! On the other hand,
My craziness remains quiet on the wide land
Of my verve. I have sometimes for being approved
By a girl or by the community, I proved
Myself and made some foolishness. I have not
Always dared to do what I thought to do a lot.

VI

Son! Certain consequences determined and certain
Good will of remaining faithful to myself again
Please me than the inconsequence. I am refused,
Along of my life, to expose me; I was fused.

VII

O Vicky! I believe that phrases deceive us;
For the language imposes us the synchronous
Logic that is not often in the life ahead;
The most precious is what lives informulated.

VIII

Son! I could not oust from me all reticences,
Reserves of the morality all modesties,
Fearful hesitations, that make pleasure-seeking
Afraid and predispose the heart to the ruing
After the decline of flesh. I was lived by
The interior springtime where effects of high
Echoes, all the hatchings, and the florescences
That I had naturally met on my paces.

IX

Vicky! My look smiles at a frank and blind love. Kindness
Is only an irradiation. My ruthless
Heart yields at all and specially you for only
Effect of being joyous. I thus feel in me
The imperious obligation of being
Joyful. But all joy appears to me revolting
That taks possession at the expense of others.
You give me the joy and you learn me good manners.

X

O son! There on the land many dense worries,
Many constaints, many horrors and distresses
That the happy man cannot remind it without
Taking shame of his rapture; what gives me the doubt.
My bliss is to augment this one of others. Then
I need bliss of each other for being often
Blissful. I am telling, for the felicity
That takes bound or leap over the misery,
I don't need it. A richness that deprives others,
I don't need it. If my cloth denudes my patness,
I will go naked. Ah! You keep table open!
What will make the beauty of our wedding again.

No 55

Beauty of life

I

I never admire the beauty when it does not
Know that it is beautiful. My magnificat:
The perfect possession only proves itsel by
The gift; this is what makes the beauty of well-nigh
Americans. All that you do not know to give
Possesses you. Without sacrifice of pensive
And common love, there is no resurrection. And
Nothing will be blowing up only by offrande1.

II

O fruit full of flavor! May the morality
Envelop! I need to make abandon of me
For sprouthing. This is in shunning that all virtue
Completes itself. All my being belongs to you.
What breeze of sea or of hill that carries you there!
Black bird, shivering and taking wings, you appear
And you stay on this extreme escarped rock also
Far that the existing time can bring you. You show
That you advance; and with all your respects
You dart forth in the future or in the prospects.

III

Fear of stumbling cramps our minds on the hill
Of logic. There is logic, what escapesfrom real
Logic. The illogism thus irritates me,
But the exces of the logic naturally
Tires me out. There are those who reason, and there are
Those who let others have reason.this is to par2
Defect of the logic that I see very clear,
And that all the things to me normally appear.

IV

This is the gratitude of my heart that makes me
Invent God everyday. And from the sunshiny,
I am amazed to be; I endlessly wonder.
Why does raising of a pain bring less joy, less laughter
Than the end of a joy then causes me the most
Of pain. This is what makes me look like a ghost.

V

This is in the regret you remember a bliss
Whose God just removes from you and that you feel miss.
Whereas he does not arrive to recall to pains
That are spared by you. This is that it maintains
That humankind supposes to be really
Happy as all the others, as you and as me.

VI

A sun of happiness is due to each creature
According that his sense and his heart can nurture
It. So few as they take away from me, I fly
Into rage. I forget if I reclaim the high
Life before to be; but at this very moment,

All are due to me; else I become violent.

VII

This state of happiness, if you do not know how
To keep it, do not too much search to reach it now.
It appeared, after having kicked the selfishness,
That3. I had made flow out such a plentiness
Of joy from my heart that I can heap all others
With it. Thus I understand that the best teaching
Is example. I seize my bliss as a nice calling.

VIII

The life may be more beautiful that the men do
Not agree it. The bliss is the love, the true
Compassion, the reason. Oh! I too prudently
Lived until now. Nevertheless, one must be
Without law for discarding the natural law,
All that can make the humankind happy and braw.

IX

Ah! My birth did not call me to the throne of crimes!
Oh! my friends! For sleeping so tranquil, we sometimes
Must have certain dreams. It is too cruel to live
In a mansion of fairies where murmur active
Songs of angels and where the gospels of Jesus
Have been read, to sleep in it, and to wake up thus
In a shanty stained with blood, full of rubbishes
Of weapons, with terrible specters and dummies.

X

O shame! O excess of misery! If there are
Laws in the world, if some justice exists so far
On the earth, because there are true and sacred guys,
I will bend myself until ground to their eyes.

XI

When the formation of masses will be enough strong
To stop children smiling when their parents belong
To the sobs. Is the criminality a law
Of the nature? What they call the love and the braw
Virtue, is this quite the cloth that they put on
Every Sunday for going to church as a fun?

XII

How the happiness of humankind is a dream,
This is quite hard; how the is blood-stream,
Irrevocable, endless and impossible
To change. Why do the worldwide and invincible
Diplomats who work for the world look around them
Instead of looking around the people ad rem.

XIII

Having certain dreams is the life of all the men!
The strongest have represented theirs so often
With all their powers, and nothing change them; they fit.
Their imaginations were a tree full of neat
Saps; whence the buds easily metamorphosed it
In flowers; and then the flowers in exquisite
Fruits; soon the fruits ripened by a beneficient
Sun; and when they were ripe, they detached themselves and
Fell on the ground without truly losing on land

An unique grain of their virginal dust. Alas1
The beautiful dreams of weakest are trees of brass
Very difficult to nourish, that they wather
Them with the bitter tears for making them proper.

XIV

A bloody injury can engender other
Hurts in the bodythe sanest. But the better
Drops of kisses of a mother often appear
As a sweet-smelling plant that just heals all the scare
Hurts. The art, this divine flowers, sometimes will need
Some manures for manuring the soil so arid.

XVI

The nations quite peaceful and happy have sometimes
Shined of a pure clearness, but weak in all the times.
There are several cordsto the harps of angels; then
The zephyr can murmur on the weakest again,
And to pull from their soft accords or harmony
Suave and sweet; but the cord of silver only
Shake to passage of northern wind. This is the most
Beautiful and the noblest as the gold coast,
And meanwhile to touch it with a rude hand
Is very favorable for it on the strand.
1-offrande means offering. 2-par means striking. 3-that
I had made flow out, that being a conjunctive pronoun is
the complement of direct object of verb appeared.

False association

I

Fantasy is a disturbed vision. Twist then
Reality in any way, you are again
Perceiving destructively. The fantasies are
A means of making false associations and far
Attempt to obtain pleasure from them. But although
You can perceive the false associations, even though,
You can never make them real except to yourself.
You believe in what you make, do not be an elf.

II

The inappropriate use of projection or
Extension occurs when we believe that some more
Emptiness or lack existsin us, and that1 we
Are open to fill it with our instinctively
False ideas instead of truth. And I do not see
About what false associations you talked truly.

III

If the men are men rather than bears and panthers,
If they are fair, if they get used to do charters
Or justice to themselves, and that they render it
To others, what ise of laws, their discreet
Texts, the prodigious despondency of their long

Commentaries? And what is the use of the strong
　　Petition and of the possession, and all they
　　Really call jurisprudence. Try to be so gay.

IV

How so many superb men in the different
　　Exercises of peace and of impertinent
Wars would have had to dispense with! Indeed,
　　At what level of refinement and of solid
Perfection didn't they bring certain arts and sciences
　　That didn't have to be useful in the communities
As the remedies at all the pains where our own
　　Malice is the unique source! We are really done.

V

The rancors are so long and very obstinate
That the greatest sign of death in the normal state
　　Of man quite sick is the reconciliation
　　That is a sort of together motivation.
There seizures of land and removal of mines,
　　Of prison and of tortures, and also of pines;
　　But justice, laws, necessity, are on one side.
This is not a new thing to admire with what wide
　　Ferocity the men treat other men. Often,
　　I ask me if I was not in a dream again.

VI

I almost assure that the men then know better
To take action that follows them, to decipher
What is necessary to do and what is well
Necessary to tell rather than to do or tell
What is necessary. This is what is the cause
Of all misunderstanding in the worldwide laws.
How many kinds of ridicules widespread among
Men, but who by their singularity so strong
Do not draw to consequence, and have no resource
For theinstruction and for the moral course.

No 57

Difference of opinions

I

The particulars have no peace between them, and
We want to give it to the souvenir quite planned,
And to render it even eternal. Do we
See poceedings between religious so holy,
Between strongest and weakest, no public order.
Do not we see the religious communities
Starting proceedings against other communities.
Still religious. Therefore the elites or the true
Christianism, and the persons the most due
And the most engaged by a particular task
To only preach the peace to others without mask.

II

The conflicts between the presidents are only
The proceedings between the particulars, we see.
Do we pretend to change the human heart; do we
Pretend to do with our unique reasonings more
Than Christ has not completed until now encore
With his holy laws, with his great miracles and
His strong menaces, with his prodigious and planned
Promises; can we wish that the motives purely
Human are enough for our goals quite dainty.

III

We do not pretend to change the human heaert, whence
We do not pretend to banish the doifference
Of opinions, contestations, and the reverse,
By supposing that sovereigns are not perverse
Men. They must suppose as neighborings they can have
The difference of opinions even quite grave.
We propose ourselves as way of arbitratioin
For terminating conflict and provocation.

IV

I pretend to show one thing. Indeed, by taking
Truly the way of arbitration, this living
Difference of opinions would be in the next
In slightest number and also quite less perplexed.
And that way would be more convenient, quite less
Ruinous, quite less dangerous than the lawless
Way of weapons. This has to be the objective
Of all sovereigns in their thoughts so negative.

V

I uniquely bound myself to show that the way
Of violence that God gives us common with stray
Or witjh anmals must not be often preferred
To way of arbitration that we just fostered
On the reason that distinguishes us with beasts.
This way supposes to beour permanent feasts.

VI

Judges do not follow wraths of parties, they do
Not expose themselves to disturb whose they have to
Be the protectors; nothing made more resentment
To heaven than spectacle of an innocent
Who would be afflicted by the proper judges.
That would carry the fear, also the anguishes.

VII

The judges have other ways for discovering
The crimes that are to examine with a brimming
Application the hates, the inimities, and
The interests, and the other things that can pretend
Or can be the causes and the normal motives;
Otherwise, there are so many alternatives.

VIII

Or it is enough, according to the sentence
Of judges, of having committed a crime whence
For being condemned of having committed it;
Judges must do mproceedings of all nature fit1.
Alas! The nature is also weak, and also
Corrupted that it is in its origin; so
It is possible that the men the wisest and
The judges become of scoundrels quite very bland.

IX

It bis possible that judges let them selvesbe
Parvened by the rich against the poor specially.
It is possible that judges follow passion
Of a powerful accusator in fashion,
And that2 they consult with him the ways of twisting

The procedure with his own will as a fair thing.

X

It is impossible that they do not want to take
Proofs that go to discharge of the accused unjake.
It is possible that they refuse all the lights
That one gives them, and that3 they affect the rights
To hide the criminals, as we often see it
Everyday in the world. Nothing is so concrete.

XI

All these possibilities are all truer too
As this is the bible that told them with its few
Terrible reproaches that it addressed often
To the corrupted judges: "How long will you then
Stop judging unfairly? And how long will you stop
Favoring the tue evils who are in the top.

XII

As it would be unjust to condemn the judges
On these possibilities, and although this is
Expressed in the bible: it is also unjust
That judges condemn whoever on the discussed
And similar possibilities. This again
Appears in the worldwide convention so often.

XIII

This does not surprise me if the diplomatic
Judges of United Nations condemn a chic
Man without blame, about only it could open
The door for a murder without the judges then
Know if he has effectively opened it.

How many times left so thatearth will be complete.
1-fit being a qualificative adjective of nature is placed after the
common noun because of theb rhyme..2-and that they cnsult,
that being a cojunctive pronoun is the complement of direct
objectbof verb is. And thatthey affect, that being a conjunctive
pronoun is the complement of direct object of verb is.

No 58

Misdeamenors

I

The sentiments that I propose you are today
Those of all the honest men.they, by anyway,
Abandon all the old chimeras to the whole
Masses. For understanding, we must have a soul.
They do the mysterious where there is no grand
Mystery. And then for letting us understand
What is understand by itself; and the spirit
Of discernment is the way the surest anf fit.

II

After the spirit of discernment, what there is
The rarest to the world or to certain countries,
Those are the diamobds and the pearl. All people
Of village admire this place by their principal
Thoughts; nevertheless, this is only a full swing
Of thought enshrined by a pure rubbish quite living.
A touchstone quite sure traduction so precious
Of Theophrastusthat then comes to give us,

III

There is only to know how the simplicity
Of Theophrastus was found poor by majority
Of guys pretended of having good taste, to great

Surprise and to great scandal of so passionate
Worshippers of ancients, and knowing at the same
Time how the vast public has preferred to the tame
Characters of Theophrastus the delicious
Notions of moderns that gave tradition to us.

IV

Montaigne, Larochfoucault, Pascal did not order
Of series of abstract formulas. Moreover,
They have an original manner of judging
The life; each of them sees the human functioning
By a side that one had never then apperceived.
For the reviewers, before all have been conceived.

V

Labruyere, on the other side, only discovers
Truths of details; he shows ridicule of manners
Or modes, the dislike of vices, the injustice
Of opinion, the vanity of all propice
Attachments of the human beings in a line
Quite well-defined for our intelligence so fine.

VI

These scattered views do not drive him to a unique
Idea; he tries thousand rails, do not cut a quick
Path; so many true remarks, he does not thus form
A togetherness. He gives advice quite conform
To each age, to each condition, to each passion,
But never to the humanity in ration.

VII

We american people bring in us the germ
Of the profound transformations that, in the firm
Twenty-first century, will renew all aspects.
This will be our divine mission full of prospects.

VIII

This is an epoch where the generous souls start
To say that the search of common welfare or part
Is the only task of all the humanity.
Oh! at last, there will be no nationwide army.

IX

When a lecture raises the minds and it inspires
Them the noble and generous feelings as lyres,
They do not need to look for another ruler
For judging the bottom of important ledger.

X

There atre misdemeanors that are such only by
Their starts and in their source an abuse or a nigh
Bad usage, and that1 are always less pernicious
In their outfits and in the common practice thus
Than a principle faireror than a custom
More reasonable, and that2 just bring the wisdom.

XI

We see a variety of misdemeanors
That we can correct by the change or by orders,
that are wrong, strongly dangerous or so risky,
that bring feud in the middle of society.

XII

There are other wings quite hidden as of trashes
In a sewer, buried under the disgraces,
Under secret. Wise men doubt if it is better
To know those misdeeds or to ignore them further.

XIII

We sometimes tolerate in a state a very
Great tort, but that diverts a million of tony
Errors or of inconvenients that all would
Be inevitable, hopeless, and quite not good.

XIV

There are torts that suit well-being and advantage
Of each family. There are others that ravage,
Tease or shame of family, but that accommodate
Conservation of the machinery of state.

XV

War exists since the antiquity; it has been
In all centuries:and we have always seen
It filling the society with the widows,
With the orphelans, with the disease and the blows.

XVI

All the times the men come between them to plunder
Each other, to burn each other, to kill each other,
To slaughter one another. They invent in part
The nice order that they call military art.

XVII

They joined to practice of the orders the glory,
The most solid reputation, have since truly
Gone so better of century in century
On way of killing each other mutually.

XVIII

From the constant injustice of men the war came,
As well as the necessity where the same
Men where found themselves to give them the masters
Who fixed their rights, their pretentions and their tempers.
1-and that are always less pernicious, that being a relative pronounof
misdemeanors is the subject of verb are. 2-and that just bring the
wisdom, that being a relative pronoun is the subject of verb bring.

No 59

I

Do not have a grudge at men in seeing their pride,
Their hardness, their ingratitude and their wrong side,
Their injustice, the self, the self-love the neglect
Of others. They make their nature so imperfect.

II

We see that the men change their cloths,their languages,
Their outfits, the norms; they change their taste and senses.
They keep their ways always bad, firm in the misdeed
Or in the indifference for virtue so mid.

III

One does not compel the malignant souls that they
Have to sweetness, the suppleness, and the fair play;
They don't lack them; they use them as trap to surprise
The wises, and just for valorizing their guise.

IV

Basically such man in himself can't define
Himself: too many thingsthat are out of him twine
Him, change him, move him deeply. It is not truly
What he is or what he really appears to be.

V

Modesty is not or is confused with a thing
Quite different of self; and if we are taking
It for an interior sentiment that then
Demeans man to his own eyes, and that is again
A supernatural virtue that we still call
Humility that the church tries us to recall.

VI

Verily, the modesty only tends to do
That no one suffers from it; it is a virtue.
Exterior that adjusts our conservations,
Our eyes, our talks, our tones of voice, our sensations,
And that1 makes the man act with others openly
And quite exterioly such as it should be.

VII

You tell that we need to be modest; the well-born
Persons do not ask more: do only that the sworn
Men do not encroach on thoser who yield by the true
Modesty, and do not ruin those who then subdue.

VIII

We have to procure modest cloths, it is encore
True. The persons of merit desire nothing more;
People want the finery, one gives it to them,
They are avid of fills2, one shows to themthe gem3.
1-and that makes the man act, that being a relative pronoun
of vitue is the subject of verb makes. 2-fills means superfluity
in the improper sense.. 3- gem means treasure and pearl.

No 60

Egoism

I

The one who understand and protects the other
Will not suffer the doubts for choosing, either
The imperfection that the desire does notice.
His body will renew the spotless prejudice.
For the pleasure of seeing, the eyes have not seen
Such beauty either wonderful exploits so clear.

II

The taste that makes me look for a true lifestyle
In this town is as a taste of angels to unvile
Wedding lamb. My meals have a kind of natural
Delice; my finance progress quite in a way normal.
Water of rock of America is again
Always fresh: and then our taste that is so often
Contrary will never taste the sweet bitterness
Either the bitter sweetness. All are in gladness.

III

So weak, I cannot approach frm my eyes the eye
Of sky. Still quite dazzled, I melt into my shy
Soul for seeing the great soul of the world; just to
Know what persons does not know and person so due
Cannot know; what the ear did not hear, and then what

The eyes were incapable of seeing. My fat
Senses have no sense, again personal feeling
Quickly comes to fly aways as the end of spring.

IV

The egoism is a metaphysical
Variety of malady so critical.
It is a disease that, as influenza, falls
On all the people in the world. It has its galls1.
Preacher runs round a ring formed by his own talent,
Falls in an admiration of it, does enchant
Itself and exploits the religious relations
That he has with others by his presentations.

V

Beware of preacher who says: "I am on the eve
Of a revelation of God." Do not believe.
The religious literatures have the stately2
Examples, and if we run over our privy
List of poets, philosophers, philantropists
And critics, we will find them injected by grists
Of the dropsy and of elephantiasis
Which we ought to havetapped. And this the disease.

VI

This goiter of egoism is frequent among
The notable persons that we infer some strong
Necessity in nature of which it subserves.
When a person is egoist, he all conserves.

VII

Egoism has its root in the cardinal
Necessity by which each individual
Persists to be what it is. Additionally,
The individuality is not only
Consistent with religion or divine culture,
But also it is the basisof it by nature.

VIII

It is very far from us that time of the first
Gospel where church, again animated at first
By holy spirit, thaught to kings, to presidents,
To people not to love the war; it taught to gents
The humility, fraternity, charity,
Sublime abnegation, heroic constancy!

IX

It is far fromus that time where godly servants
Or the Christians, inspired and sublimed, pulled down tyrants
With a hand, and with the other they really rose
The persecuted as a perfumed flower of rose!

X

Those times of Saint Francis and Saint Clare, where pastors
And priests of Jesus Chrits, worthy as successors
Of Peter and Paul, had no other ambition
Than to pull the people out of bad derision,
Of conflicts, of hoplessness and of misery,
Instead of embracing the world of a godly
Love the most terrible, the most incredible,
Instead of preaching a love quite ostensible.

XI

Yes, it is far from us that glorious time where
The religious leaders, born of poor immense there
At Capernaum, and full of celestial light,
Truly recognized among the men other right
Distinction than this one of virtue or of power
To which the morals only can give right, further.

XII

Because all the men are children of same father
Who all created them for the joy and rapture.
Alas! People do not find in the religious
Leader a second father who consoled them, thus
Who directed them, who support them, and who
Loved them, who understood them, who made them real, true.

XIII

People do not find in the religious preacher
And inside churches this devoted and tender
Friend who only made them hear the true messages
Of love and of hope; messages of amities.

XIV

People do not find in the religious preacher
The kind-hearted voice that echoed in their tender
Souls as a divine harmony, who, instead of
Possessions on-earth, showed the sky above
All, who by of words filled them with courage,
Of strength, of joy, and who with a body language
Transforms in delices their most nefarious
Hurts, their tribulations the most preposterous.

XV

Alas! There he enters himself in the system
Of exploitation, who makes cause common idem
To tyrants, who gives them his sacred loyality
After abolishing slavery by charity,
And welcomes the servitude and exploitation
By ambition of gain and of reputation.

XVI

There he reasserts the value of selfishness
And of greed, reminds only to do a measureless
Part in the pillages of the nation, only
To have a good place to sun of authority.

XVII

He pretends to be lamb and makes himself vampire
At same time. He drinks sweath and blood of his nigher
Worshippers. He always grows fat at the substance
Of the servants; he applies all his performance.

XVIII

That hideous Polyp has manufactured yet
A multitude of alike ruiners so coquet,
Susceptible at their turn of manufacturing
A multitude of others; all are adhering
At the same trunk, immense and impenetrable
Network in which worshippers spo amiable
Are oppressed and tied so as to entangle then
Themselves in the least movement that they dare again
To do; this horrible social phenomena,
That fire could destroy, start to invade this terra.
1-galls means malices. 2-stately means eminent.

Human machine

I

Strange regard for all the principle! Strange justice
That is everywhere the right of strongests in malice!
Oh! this spectacle is so hard to see! Such is
Depotism that hangs over societie.

II

The people, stunned and degraded, were everywhere
Serfs or slaves. Or for telling better with a fair
Word, it exists two classes of men: oppressors
And oppressed, executioers and sufferers.

III

Each land has its lord who then knows other laws than
His interests, his position, his wim and his plan,
Who wages war endlessly on his homebodies
For looting, stealing and stripping their ressources.

IV

What they name the people is only a machine
That they forcefully push to the war and to mean
Conflicts between each other, thatl they thus submit
Them at all kinds of ordeals and bumps so unneat.

V

Those are them, the people, who under the nickname
Of villains in the shanty town, and in the tame
Cities and the towns: the middle classes then pay
From their blood and their ressources the gay
Extravagances of their owners and of all
Misfortunes that happen to their owners so tall2.

VI

The people only exist for that; they have no
Other destination that keep alive and so
Warm to feet of the pride and of the luxury.
There are only good to be flouted and very.........3.

VII

God had created them only for the harms and
The work, only for the burdens to stand,
Only for the loads today. He told them: "Grow and
Multiply for the profit of yourlord and grand
Owners, and keep yourselves very honored
When he will deign to approach himself of your lored
Wife or your girl. Live and die for him. Lavish
Your blood in the fight for the defense of his knavish
Rights, and your sweath in the wild fire of the furrow
For his well-being ; you are his possession,oh!
You belong to him; his will is your law. Do not
Stand up to his words; you are a thing in his cot."

VIII

If this is not language of God, this is about
The one of the preacher who lavishedly points out
Himself in this distribution that he had made

With the substance of people, and who is not afraid
Of recommending specially to pay tiths or
The taxes. For the tith, this is less thing or more.

IX

In the past the Jews payed the tith in the temple
Of Jerusalem. This were a free principle
Of voluntary oblationsof worshippers
Passed toi the state of tax; this is all, o preachers!
What there were more hideous, this were not to be
Able to possess nothing with sureness, really
Not to can say:" This money, this propriety
Belong to me. All belong to God normally."

X

A villainous does not need jewel or airplane,
And then he is born for going on his profane
Feet. The preacher truly needs oxes for plowing.
Jewelries on the body of a worshipping
Villainous, what a sacrilege! There is no pride
That fits a villainous better than the wide
Menaces on condemnation or on the hell;
The servants being naïve obey to his spell.

XI

There will be so many of them who will regret
System of brigandages where justice was yet,
As we see it, only the right of the strongest
Where the ravages and the horrors of longest
Exploitation, spreading itself on all sidesof earth,
Make angels of sky weep on the earth without mirth.

XII

I tell nothing about taxes of the buying
Back of human soul; and this other inventing
Domain, founded by the priests and by the pastors
On the human consciences and idolators
In a century of superstition and crimes,
Successfully becomes productive all the times.

XIII

For the money certain believers have been the
Forgiven for the passed sins, and even again
For those ones that they keep for themselves toi commit
In the future. God loves all that is illicit.

XIV

While the money does procure such perogatives,
Judge if the preacher makes mistake or deceives
Himself to steal, to pillage, to use to his good
Advantage the ressources of servant so due.
1-that they thus submit, that being a relative pronoun of machine
is the complement of direct object of verb submit. 2- tall
means high. 3-the dots of suspensions replace humiliated.

No 62

Religious theory is a tale

I

You never only think of avoiding that tope
System. Nothing will brighten up the dawn of hope
To the hell. Would God have uninterruptedly
Moved away from you his grace, his clemency?

II

The one who has sinned also suffers endlessly.
Grace of God puts its office to sky quite bonny;
He tends to open out his anger and his justice
Without partiality and without prejudice.

III

The corrupted air does not have its corrupting
Breath, and does not make its office of alluring
Elements to the hell. Numb and despaired, this is
No death that is for its sea the port of deluges.

IV

Such as we see to the furnace appearing
The numbs, as the son of heaven have the hearing
Of their master to face: Jesus the sharp picture.
And the other children of the hell by nature
Have certain features in common with the great prince

Belzebul veritable picture, they convince.

V

I say nothing about the increase in power
Of religions thet put their power in the flower
Of service of their interests and of their passion.
I say nothing about the chaste book in fsashion
That permits them to make justice according to
Their follies, that gives them the faculty so due
Of reparing all the offences by the quick
Financial compensations to which the fabric
Of the superstition comes to exaggerate
By the judicial ordeals quite obstinate.

VI

Religion is the suggestion from certain best
Thoughts that a philosopher has a range of strongest
Affinities through which he can then modulate
The violence of any master-tones that state
Or have a droning preponderance in its scale.
Theory of religion is only a tale.

VII

The religion redresses its balance, put it
Among its equal, its superiors, its fit.
It revives the delicious sense of sympathy
And warms it of the dangers of frivolity.

VIII

The best heads that even existed in this sphere,
Periclkes, Plato, Julius Ceasar, Shakspear,
Goethe, Milton, were well-read, and universally
Educated men, and quite too wise to really
Undervalue letters. Their opinions have weight,
Because they had means of thus admitting the straight
Opposite opinion; what is so different
Of biblical writers who did not stand judgment.

No 63

Lover of an instant

I

O you for whom I write and I called in the past
A name that appears today too plaintive at last:
My girl. Today, I call you: my lover, my art.
Do not admit anything plaintive in your heart.
Try to obtain from me what just makes the complaint
Inutile. Do not implore what you can acquaint
Or obtain to other. You lived, this is my turn.
This is in you that youth goes on your concern.

II

What deserves to be, and also what would deserve
Not to be. How to part this one from that one, my verve!
Odette, do you want to look for the salvation
Of the humanity in the admiration
Of the past. This is in pushing out of the way
What has stopped serving in the past of the old day
That the progress normally becomes possible.
My darling, to me do not be impossible.

IV

Perfect possession proves itself by talent. Too,
All that you do not tempt to give possess you.
Nothing only blooms by the gift. What you pretend

To protect in you atrophies, you understand.
The gratitude is so sweet and it is to me
Neededly sweet of loving and the least footsie1
Of air raises a mercy in my heart. The need
Of gratitude leans me to do what is good deed.

V

This state of joy, if you do not know to maintain
It, do not pursue to attainit; it is vain.
Do not pretend to deny what could then tarnish
Limpidity oif your character so lavish.
Oh! the day where I parvene to persuade me
That I will not need to be happy, gaiety
Would start living in me. The day where I really
Prevailed that I needed nothing to be happy.

VI

O Odette, my lover! After you give a blow
Egoism, it seems that you let reflow
Or spurt in my heart such an abundance of joy
That I arrive to drink all others as a soy.
You let me know that best teaching is illustration
Quite normal. I guess my joy as a vocation.

VII

Faster is the crossing, unimaginative
Is your inconsideration, more impulsive
Is your flight, more sudden is your embrace! Lover
Of an instant, for what reason would I ever
Embrace less lovingly what I know that I will
Not to be able to hold on my faith very leal?

VIII

I only seize the words by the wings. Is this you,
Woodpigeon of my joy? Ah! Through the azure, do
Not fly away another time! My loving bird,
Lay here and have time to catch your breath; this is heard!
Spring full of pertness, I implore your clemency!
My indecisive thought driftingwith the summery
Current of your breeze. Drink my heart without defense.
O congested route! In it, there is no offense.

IX

Thousand luminous cords cross and there come to tight
In my heart. From thousand foresights, I weave a right
Miraculous cloth. Toward the steam of my heart,
I saw you. Through you, my lips hang themselves beneath.
1-footsie means caress.

No 64

Devout dreamer

I

O my brothers! Thanks to heaven, there we are free
From all this frightened device of philosophy:
We can be men without being learned, dispensed
To ruin our life to study of moral unsensed1
We have at this lower price a guide more assured
In this wide maze of human conductor or guide-word2

II

We have to recognize this guide, to follow it.
And if it speaks to all the hearts quite so discrete,
Why are there so few people who listen it or
Who receive its generous messages once more.
Eh! This is that guide specially speaks to us
Language of the nature; all make us forget thus.

III

The conscience is shy, it likes the retirement and
The peace. The crowd and the noise just frighten or send
Chills to it. The prejudices that they make it
Rise core its cruel foe; it makes a quick exit.

IV

The loud voice of prejudices is suppressing
The voice of the conscience and just stop it having
It heard. The fanatism dares to falsify
It and to command the crime in its name so high.

V

The voice of conscience repels by dint of being
Rejected; it does not take to us; by adding,
It does not answer us after we desprise it.
It is so worthy of reminding it than it
Is worthy to ignore it. It is a true guide.
The religion dismantles in us all its pride.

VI

From what can I be guilty by worshipping God
According to the lights that he gives to my mod
Spirit according to the nice sentiment
That inspires to my heart and to my sentient.

VII

From what a saneness of morals cannot I pull
Without it a good usage from my faculties quite full?
From what creed useful to man and honorable
To God can I pull a doctrine favorable?

VIII

Let us see the spectacle of the nature, let us
Listen the inside voice. And did not God tell thus
Everything to our eyes, to our understandings,
To our conscience, to our judgments, to our feelings.

IX

What will the men tell us? Their revelations
Degrade God, in giving human aspirations
Or human passions to him. Far to enlighten
The notions of supreme Being. And I often
See that the particular doctrines make them more
Complicated. We cannot see the truth encore.

X

Particular doctrines are far to enoble
The notions of God. They then make them ignoble
In dignity. Whence to the inconceivable
Mysteries that gird them, they are affordable
To augment some absurb conditions that make men
Proud, intolerant, cruel, instead so often
Of establishing the peace on the entire earth;
They bring the weapons and the fire instead of mirth.

XI

Many pastors told me that I need a divine
Revelation for learning to the menthe fine
Way whose God wanted toi be served. They openly
Teach with proof the diversity of kinky
Or bizarre denominations that they then
Instituted; they do not even see again
That this diversity comes from the fantasy
Of revelations or figment of prophecy.

XII

As soon as people realize to make God speak,
Each one made him speak to his method quite so chic
And made him tell what they wanted. Do not mix

Rite of religion with religion. What a mix!

XIII

The cult that God requires is this one of heart; and
That one is always uniform when it is grand
And sincere. Whence this is to have a vanity
Very crazy to imagine that God truly
Takes a so great interest in the form of the cloth
Of priests or pastors, of the order of their troth
Or words and all genuflexions that they would
Pronounce on the holy chair that does not seem rude.

XIV

A devout leader is a dreamer, a leader
Who always stands on all his dream and who ever
Forgets that he is enough close to ground. By sooth,
God wants to be praisedin spirit and in truth,
Specially in the virtue of the poverty,
Of the humility and of simplicity.

XV

Indeed, this duty is for all the religion,
For all the doctrines, for all counties or regions,
For all men. As for outer cult, if it is then
Uniform for the good order, this is again
Purely an affair of police. Let us see, we
Do not need the revelation for that, truly.
1-unsensed is placed after the common noun because of
rhyme and means foolish, ridiculous. 2-guide-word is not
written at plural because of rhyme and means supervisor.

No 65

The seed of virtue

I

I have so much thought about the manners of men,
For not telling particurlarly the hidden
Influence of that first movement on the long end
Of their lives. If I hide or feign to understand
Nothing, that presiudes itself on my weakness; thinking
To throw dust in their eyes, I am considering
Me to have a low idea. I am a party
Of their loss. If I try to bring them back, really,
They are not going to listen me; then I will
Become annoying, odious, akward, unreal
And unbearable; they are not going to take
Any moment to get rid of me as a fake.

II

I only have a logical party to take,
This is to make them countable of their mistake
And of tjheir actions to themselves, to guarantee them
at least some surprises of the error, ad rem,
to show them openly the dangers whose they are
edged; this is by light we need to stop them so far.

III

For leading a dreamer, we must take opposite
Of all that we could have made for leadind a chit.
What we told means nothing if we did not prepare
To tell it. This is not like that whose human hearts share.
Before sowing, we need to plow the soil: the seed
Of virtue hardly develops in some arid
Lands; and we have need of a long preparation
For helping it to take root with calculation.

IV

One thing that makes the predications the most
Innefficaciousis that they make them almost
Indifferently to every group of people
Without discernement, without choice and principle.

V

Do not fight the desires of priests and of pastors
With rigidness; do not suffocate their ardors
And their imaginations; and guide them for fear
As they do not engender the monster. Be clear;
Talk to them about love, about woman, about
Pleasures; act like they find in your talkings without
Hesitation a charm that then flirts their young hearts,
Their young souls, their senses as some beautiful arts.

VI

Then do not scare if our conversations bother
Them. They make us speak more than we do not prefer.
O ministers of God! Take back authority
That you want to depose at a moment truly
That it is important to me the most than it

Left you; you had it bymy weakness so discreet;
Now you have it by my will, and it will be more
Sacred. This is my messages to you encore.

VII

O God! Defend me against all the enemies
Who besiege me, specially the adversaries
That I carry with me, and that1 betray me. Watch
Your book so that it remains worthy at your match.

VIII

I want to obey your rules, I always
Want them; this is my constant will. If all the days
I disobey you, this will be despite me; give
Me the strength to protect me against my active
Passions that make violence to me; stop me
Being their slave; and compel me daily to be
My own master in obeying not to my sense,
But to my reason and to my intelligence.

IX

The miniters of God do not know with what zeal
The senses drive their resemblances in the real
Abyss of vices, under appeals of pleasures.
Whence they clearly do not have of abject creatures.

X

The ministers of God do not repudiate
Their faith, but how much time perhaps they expiate
To have given it! How man times they then curse
The one who loves them, considers him as perverse.

1-and that betray me, that being a relative pronoun
of adversaries is the subject of verb betray.

No 66

Beauty of nature

I

On a summery evening, I am just going
To take a walk at Coney Island where shining
Horizon completely will let see the sunset,
And there we will get to examine the quiet
Objects that naturally tend to make that place
So agreeable of setting. What a nice face!

II

Tomorrow we return at the same place before
The sunrise for breathing the fresh air. Furthermore,
We will see it piling up from a great distance
By dabs of fire, it will point ahead our presence.

III

The fire augments and the orients appears quite
In fire. At their brightness we expect the skylight
Before it appears; at each instant we long for
Seeing it appearing, at last we see it more.

IV

A shiny point goes up as a flesh and fills all
Space; the veil of darkness does with draw and does fall.
The verdure the takes in the night a new freshness;

The beginning of day that shines down on it; yes!
The first ray that gilds seems coered by a sparkling
Network of dew that reflkects light, color painting.

V

The different birds in choir join each other
And together give extolment to the father
Of the life. In this moment no one remains
So quiet; their chirpings so weak are very slower
And softer than the end of the day and ever
They feel languid of a pacific alarm day.

VI

The support of those objects bring to the sense
An impression of freshnessthat sems to influence
Or to penetrate until the soul. There is here
A half-hour of enchantment to which no sincere
Man resists; a spectacle so great, so bonny,
So delicious, does not leave the calm completely.

VII

Full of enthusiasm that the spectacle
Tends to show, the teacher as a miracle
To communicate it to the present children.
He believes toi move them by making them often
Attentive to the feelings whose they are having
Been moved in themselves as quite inside their being.

VIII

True comedy! This is in the heart of the man
That the spectacle of nature exists more than
We imagine. For seeing it, we must feel it;
We must understand it and we must inspire it.

IX

The child perceives the objects, but he cannot see
Any connection that links them naturally;
He cannot hear the sweet harmony of their concert.
We have an experience that the child has not
Acquired; we have feelings that he has not a lot
Tested for feeling the compound impression that
Results at the same time of his feelings so flat.

X

If he has not longtime gone all over empty
Enjoyments, if ardent sands have not burned his pretty
Feet, if the suffocating reverberation
Of rocks hit by the sun in its fulguration
Has never oppressed him, how will he digustate
The fresh air a morning quite bonny and great ?

XI

How will the brightness of the day break, the watery
Steam of dew, the perfume of flowers, the beuty
Of verdure, the limp and delicate promenade
On the lawn enchant the sense of child or of lad?

XII

How will the song of birds cause a voluptuous
Emotion to him, and if the accents of muss,
Of love, of enjoyment and of accessory
Are still unfamiliar to him completely?

XIII

With what passions will he see appearing a so
Nice day, if his imagination cannot show
Or draw to him the objects that he perceives,
With those that one can fill it, he never conceives?

XIV

At las how will contemplate the gracefulness
Or the beauty of wonderful things so less
Of the nature, if he then pretends not to see
Hand that takes care of decorating it?

XV

O brothers! Do not keep to the child of talkings
That cannot hear. It is not matter of feelings
Either of taste. Continue to be clear, tender;
The time comes soon to take another palaver.

XVI

My son raises for living in the community;
He will not live among wises, but with crazy
People; he must know their craziness, and since
This is by them that they want to be guided in prince.

No 67

Religious illusion

I

What is the most ridiculous than a great
Lord becomes beggarly who carries in his straight
Poverty the real prejudices of his birth,
This is quite a beggar who only dreams his mirth?

II

What is the vilest than a rich who turns out
To be imporverished, feels appeared without doubt
To be the last of man by reminding disdain
That people owe to be poverty quite so vain.

III

What does this luxurious idiot who then
Does not know how to use himself become, who even
Only puts his heart in what is strange to him?
This idiot normally comes to be so dim.

IV

May they honor as much as they will want this king
Quite so defeated who wants to be burying
Often himself in furious under the fragments
Of his throne; I see that in his crown he laments.

IV

No father can then transmit to his son the right
To be useless to his chuns, this is not polite.
The one who eats in the idleness what one had
Not gained himself steal it, one is much as bad
And a path that the state pays for doingnothing
Does not differ from a brigand who, according
To me, lives at the cost of passer-by. Can you
Imagine that this form of waste is not so new.

VI

Working is anessential duty for vital
Man. For all idle citizen is a rascal.
How would we disdain the baseness and the vices
Whose we need to subsist without sacrifices.
I see that we only depended on wealth, and
Now they depend on the riches and on the grand......1

Vii

We only make worse our slavery and we surcharge
It with our grief. Without being free from our charge,
This is our form of poverty; this is the wont state
Where the man can fall; this is the way we call fate.

VIII

For living instead of having recourse to hig
Knowledges that are done for nourishing the eye
And the soul, not the body; if we have recourse
To our hands and and to the the usage or to resourse
That we can make of them, all the difficulties
Disappear without certain assiduities.

IX

All the games then come to be useless; the resource
Is ready at time of using it; the resource,
The probity and the honorare not longtimes
An obstacle to the life eitherto our times.

X

We need not to be coward and liar ahead
The lords; pliant and sycophant ahead ill-bred
Rascals; vile indulgentof all people; stealer
Or borrower, what is about the same matter.

XI

The opinion of others do not reach us. How
Many rascals manage the so great affairs now,
It does not matter to us; that does not stop us
Being honest persons and having delicious.........2

XII

In my first writings I captivate myself more
To ruin the prestige of illusion that encore
Gives us stupid admiration for instruments
Of our miseries and to correct these contents
Of deceitful estimation that make us honor
Some pernicious talents and scorn some useful favor.

XIII

These forces of religious illusion that let
Us think everywherethat human species is yet
Better, wiser and happier in his primitive
Constitution; right now blind, miserable and
Evil as it goes away from it; this is panned.

XIV

The religious illusion is to correct
The human judgments that it still finds imperfect,
Just delaying the progress of our vices
And to show us there where we persue devices
Of the happiness, indeed only find on
Our ways the mistakes and miseries quite common.
The religion makes us dream the celestial
Fortunes in leaving on-earth all that essential.
What a beautiful dream or hallucination!
The religions teach us the resignation.
1-the dots of suspension replca wealthy persons.
2- the dots of suspension replace bread.

No 68

Above at first sight

I

Through my closed eyelids, your tint of marabout then
Penetrates, comes up to the shade; and it even
Wins, and the monster inside me is defeated;
It brings vigor and complexion to my flesh so dead.

II

Among all the nice words that you launch from zenith
To the earth, I catch the most charming as a myth.
I do not feel like stepping on the ground; I swing
At the end of a ray, ray of your hankering
I love you with passion, this what makes me shake.

III

Your words are more than one could shake a stick at and
Inhale and exhale with rapture the scent so bland
Of an explicable suavity being
Given off these bouquets of flowers, I swing.

IV

This is a system of principles of a bold
And wii-proportioned simplicity that you hold,
And that some ponderable blows have constantly
Tried to throw it on the ground dramatically.

V

A threatened reply would be perhaps more in line
With the truth, such as it seems to me to divine.
Collect our souvenirs as flowers so charming
In a spray to prevent them from disappearing
By theforgetting, also for making of it
A document of teaching quite so explicit.

VI

As the souvenir vanishes into thin air,
The imaginations that do not want to dare
To free themselves enjoy torevive it by some
New traits; without lying, wonder adds to handsome
Wonder, and only for this need that we have to
Believe and to admire. Your treasure is so duer.

VII

The lover tries hard to answer it, then without
Exaggerating the great discretion without doubt;
And what he brings truly new to me cannot be
Still received with an absolute security.
His chronology specially leaves so much to
Desire. Whence it is evident that he has too
Wanted to provide a meal at the devotion
Of his lover; and this is quite his emotion.

VIII

Despite you make me unhappy, I completely
Decide to abadon everything and truly
To follow you in what you order me. Indeed,
I have in my heart for you a love so lucid.

IX

O poor miserable lover! Why is your heart
Full of superfluous love? Do not surprise apart
If your heart cannot afford to speak anymore
To me in a unexpressive language encore
And even it does not have the sense of hearing
The palpitation of my heart quite so wanting.

X

Patience is pure charity and proof of virtue
And of constancy; it cannot be troubled too
Either by no suffering or by no insult.
I believe: waiting for you is not difficult.

XI

O Vicky! Let us go together for having
The infinite treasure of love and of coupling;
It is a treasure so precious and so concrete
That we are not so worthy of procuring it
In our vases so vile. This treasure, this is not
Frivolity, but this is the love and a lot.

XII

A woman who has a strong head also may be
A woman of heart or of sensibility.
O Vicky! I would not be able to hide you
What I feel. I have the impression or the clue
That you are victim of a frivolous crush or
Of a love at first sight, not true love; I implore!

No 69

A favorable attraction

Forgive me, my lass, if my talks right talks smell distress!
This is in loving I suffer, this is my stress!
It is necessary that they just smell as me
The powder of desire or powder of envy.
Divine coquette who carried my mind! Whence I see
You and me in the bosom of divinity.
It is important of dying for being quite
Virtupous; your language is right but impolite.

II

It is more cruel than all I can call tigers,
Lions and wolves, pattlesnakes and bizarre monsters:
Whence you take pleasure of laughing by killing me
And I die for loving you, my bonny lady!
The dainty games tempt our minds, reserve for our firm
Love one day to let fly at top speed the infirm
Desire that wants to be now imposed between us
Or on me. This infirm desire will be total
Between us when we will be the married couple.

III

How if among the ghosts, you think of waking me
Up, you have to put down other life. My dainty
Soul calls to heaven an enthusiasm quite
Sacred put instead of my tongue your so polite
Tongue of woman that I will use as an organ
To the celestial voice, I will be a true man.
The divine signals appeared to you for seeing
Nivce secret and draws that sky to us is giving.

IV

O Odette! You have a visible sympathy
For the things of the heaven and for the beauty
Of the nature and for the morality.
And if I amuse myself to read in your soul,
You ask me to answer to your desire quite sole.
Tell me one more time what makes you judge on my rut.
Leave me again what hope I have to take about
It; a so charming speech is thus impossible
Of hearing. May not you do what is possible.

V

I draw your heart in a difference that then
Does not swell up none of them neither destroy again
The hope; and without seeing them with a severe
Eye or to nice. You are not in atmosphere,
It seems that my confused soul refuses this joy
And finds itself tired of it; in this great and coy
Happiness I fear a reserve or a great cloy.

VI

You make appear the constant heat that your desires
Have made raise in my delicate heart like your fires.
This is not that I listen your profound breath or
A favorable attraction animates more
Your desires. This is in your nice heart I expect
Some virtuous words that look quite very perfect.
I will not forgive you if you get out of respect
For blaming my burning heat that is incorrect.
This is a flame that goes out, through lack of food.

VII

I switch on your flame for turning off mine. This is
On the earth too much justice for leaving the breeze
Of virtue in a so long torture that you tease.

VIII

This is in your happiness that I long for my
Happiness. This mark of voirtue that you apply
In our love shows me that it is just, as my sigh.

IX

The eyes and the heart so turned by the lover had
Secretely followed her steps. Both beaus become glad.
How glad I am to mirror in yoiur eyes, your spell!
You are with me, my dove! You are here, my gazelle!
My lass, you inspire me an infinite esteem;
This is why I keep you company as my dream.

X

This is glad that you feel the honor that I do
To the pleasantness of your character so due.
Nevertheless I incline myself in front of you.

XI

Is not thisyou that they call "Flower"? your nice name,
You see! I all know it by heart. This is yoiur fame!
Oh! do you know, my lover! You are my winner.
I could not stand to influence of your greater
Charms; and them I am under duress of putting
Down the arms, not the arms of the understanding.

XII

Of course, I am crasy about you and I put
At your feet the awe of my faith and bring it out.
The love I have for you has something to stun you.
How this setting is nice and clean to rendez-vous.
For you, I just want to be a so candid man
And to make me so humble as long as I can.

XIII

Your trouble adds! Senseless I am not to prepare
Excellently in your whole heart the fire-place where
This flame has to be taken fire, this flame of love
Ready to consume you; and your heart cannot shove.
Eh, well! May I spread it! I give you the joy. And
Accept the happiness that to you the skies send.

XIV

Approach yourself fearlessly; or if about my
Greatness you cannot support back splendor, do I
Carry on the field of sinople a satar. Put
Between us your shade as a veil, I will have no rut.
You are not quiet. This is quite well. I let you talk
About the union of our parents, I don't walk.

XV

Why do you want to adorn us with the renown
Of your parents? At first, try to apply our own.
Because those are them who raise us. Nobility
Of heart is better than all other nobility.
I am not among them that this principle hurts.
Quite the reverse, that flatters me; me, that diverts.

No 70

Talent of pleasing

I

Whe have talents, when we have mind, when we are
Young and pretty, when the mature-mother so far
Has given us these traits, this air, this form,this height,
These legs, these arms, this look; the heart excites the fight.
It is important to make me sensitive. Whence
You know that, I am good, I always have the sense
Quite risible. You easyli forgive a slip
Of tongue so light. Surely this mistake is not deep
And big as the moon. Odette, do not make me weep.
My angel, you agree that I am very hip1.

II

I think that this is not a pride from me; in part,
Each feels hisweight and knows his limit, his depart.
My angel, star of universe! How cute you are!
You come to muse me incomparable or par
Verses: "Like ice to sun I feel melting my soul.
The fire of helldoes not equal my fire, my whole"

III

You are the one who draws the love and my nice heart!
The author of Bug-Jagal would applaud in part
Himself toi have imagined this turn for telling:
I love. Odette, are not you this author so loving?

IV

You, my blue and red flower, a little cornflower,
A little poppy, who listen me in a half-hour
With the inclined head, without telling word! Look at
Your tint of pink, your shinning front where so much pat
Spirit rests. Odette, you smile! I have the talent
Of pleasing you, is not this? But I am gallant.

V

My talk very well; in my honor and glory,
This nice speech would have to appear in the story.
Without doubt, it could make honor at my sprit.
If I recall and wrote it! They would see in it
How I court a woman, and how I go about
It for subduing the recusants. Without doubt,
I dare to adore you. Be just, may I resist
To your charms; only for me you really exist.

VI

Ah! Do not be in state of uncertainty!
You let me see that you talk clearly, Odette!
You admit that my style is tender, generous!
I could find the happiness in yoiur heart so precious.
I see nothing than the promise to love each other
In a same tenderness or tender manner.
Come to hug me! This is a so great happiness
Of kissing the man that you love, that you caress!
1-Hip means smart.

No 71

What love inspires

I

If you could know what the love inspires! O Detty,
This is a treasure of noble feelings; fancy
Is everything; beautiful is everything
In the hearts of lovers quite very amazing.

II

It seems that sky, by a pure flame, communicate
Itself to our humble nature. Fear exaggerates
In front of those dangers that we cede at splendor
Of a heroic enthusiast and ardor.

III

I was always sincerely loving: I did it
Until last day of my life: so long it is licit
Or true that the heart remains yoiung at those who then
Have the love, and give it to their lovers often.

IV

Nothing is nobler than this alliance of value
With the gallantry distinguishing the true
Lovers, and remaining in the character
Of Americans as it should be ever.
If I make the court to a woman, this is too
The good motive; this is a thing that remains true.

V

I have reason to be severe if, as my
Father of debauchery, I abused the high
Power of the money for fear and trembling
And despair in family for satisfying.......1.

VI

If the love only diverted me from a noble
Action, as soon as it is question of my global
Glory of helping other women, no pretty
Chain will not be enough to really restrain me;

VII

Instead of a man so right, so true, so franker,
So clement, so brave, who has only another
Flaw than a heart too generous and too tender.
I tell you what is true in my words quite nicer.

VIII

Who would love better a man coward and furious
As me? Capable of fighting to traits of love thus
But as a coward shaking all his members to
The only distant noise of a fight or set-to,
Not at all loving, but not at all human,
And taking so much enjoyment to even
Kill his creature-felolows by foolishness, then.

IX

What you do not arrive to understand, tell me!
Is not it strange that you disclaim endlessly
Agaist love that is at the sametime the dainty
Consolatory and the help of human body.

X

Today, I raise my voice against false arguments
Or divorce that are the most terrible torments.
I do not think of divorce, but you must see
A councellor. Let tell you: o Detty,
You are so beautiful, so glorious of grace,
You whose my country lodges betray; on my face
Incline your looks and your rues! On me as a vile
Paria, on me who believed to be a gentile.

XI

You make me suffer everyday until my bones.
You say less for softening my pains in some zones.
It finds that it is admissible on-earth to
Walk under your loving law as it should be too.
I may breathe the air that you perfume; I want to
Wander under my steps about place that you love too.
1-the dots of suspension replce my mistress.

No 72

Crush

I

Beautiful are you, Vicky! I saw you last night
In a club that my heart lost nothing of your light
Vivacity, of your poesy, and become
Desperately loving. I saw Witzer courting
The young beauty,; and Von made you the alluring
Confidence of his love. I come here to ask you
To renounce at this marriagethat he tends to
Promise you. Vicky, I cannot lose you, it is true.

II

She told: "I am well-bred and too proud for being
Your wife, and too sprred in the life for your charming."
Why did you speak like that, Vicky? She answered me:
"You who pass in the world for having infinitely
A strong brain told yesterday that you did not, with ease,
Understand superiority of verses
On the prose; you saw people who with much lore
Put their brains to the torture for seeking rhymes for."

III

Love speaks to soul and looks for a fire-place ready
To receive its blaze. This is what to you brings me.
She said: "Your love does not speak to my heart. I like
　　To be so happier as being Jack or Mike.
I want to taste the splendor and I never reach
To find that this will be a bitter wine. on each,
Both man who is the better for my fancy style,"
　　I saw that Von is very confident a while.

IV

I told: "All are vanity! The bliss does not reside
Either in the wealth or in the splendor. Beside
All, the bliss iswholy in our hearts. We all bring
In us, if we know how to drink it, the chraming
Cup of bliss. The bliss, this nectar makes you and me
The sweetest, came from the win of flowers newly
Blooming to the side of gutters, of rays of sun,
Of murmurs of rivers, of perfumes of breeze,I shun."

V

"they smile at the nature, the trees crowned with blooming
Flowers and bait thyemselves, she told, to breath of morning."
Me, come to err with me on silvery sands, and
On the grass in flowers; come to pure spring so grand
To quench thirst of your bosom. I'm your godsend.

VI

"I learned from my mother that Saint Rock became Saint
As results of miracles, she said; and by dint
Of great actions, John Marshall became marshall. And
Grant yourself all the nice speeches as they are planned."

VII

You are sweet without weakness, magnificent
Without vanity, capable of the event
Without shunning the amusements of community,
Worthy by the purity of your customs more
Than your talent for the poetry encore
In the name of tenth Muse, and by your beauty
So ravishing of one of fourth grace, fluency.

VIII

"I learned from my ancestors the story, she said,
That life the most glorious is this one that ahead
Ends to the win of a battle, you must make it,
The sparkling as it should be possible and lit."

IX

The first day I met you, I drunk the poison that
Infects my senses and my reason, and your flat
Eyes, your characters, your talk developed in me
A love for you, and your explicable idea.
The informations that I received about you
Threw me in a frenzy. The first time I saw you,
My soul quickly received you, and thenyou carried
The happiness in my proper soul so arid.

X

"if I was young and very charming, I would not
Miss to see so much art in your conduct so pat
That I found a gentleness and a honor in that. Ah!
My Tum! By what charm, by what fatality,
Do you come to make me happy? I completely
Suffer! My body and my soul are overwhelmed
By long time of bitterness, she said, quite helmed."

XI

I see you, great field wet by the blankness of dawn,
Blue lake, I take bath in your water, and each zone
Hugs the smiling air that makes me smile at your fair......1...
Yes, permit at last that the hugs of the air,
The rays of sun and all the invitations
To the happiness mix at your motivations.

XII

"my emotions are open as a religion.
Can you understand that. All feelings in my religion
Have an infinite presence. Are not you a legion?
I hnew something the nicest, she told me, there are
Those ones that I would tell you, nothing else, my star."

XIII

I love you so much, mortal start of my soul,
Joy of my heart, joy my spirit! You are my whole.
This is you that I am singing just apropos!
You now told me that you have a crush for me also.
1-the dots of suspension replace freshness.

No 73

Arguments between husband and wife

I

Oh! the one who has a heart, and who could not make
In himself the delicious board of diverse fake
Situations, some help of ones and of others
To the union of the most charming partners
Whose the love and the virtue can make good manners.

II

You must be blissful, dear Vicky: this is the end
Of all the sensible human being; and
This is the first desire that the nature imparts
Us, and the only that never leaves us as our parts.

III

But where is the bliss? Who knows it? Each one looks for
It, he does not find it. I use life to therefore
Pursue it and I will die without reaching it;
And meanwhile the religious live by faith behind it.

IV

I only know that by making you happy,
I am certain to be so. By making lovely
And useful search for you, I make it common for
Both of us. This is what lovely man wants encore.

V

Much as we ignore what we have to do, wisdom
Consistson remaining in the inaction from
Looking for the happiness without knowing where
It is; this is to expose ourselces to get clear
Of it; this is to run so many contrary
Rocks that there are some routes so thatwe get lost truly.

Vi

In the troubled heart where ardor of well being
Keeps us, we like to mislead us to be looking
For it, we do nothing to pursue it; and then
We have to get out of the place where we can
Know it, and we cannot thus come back to it. Whence
With same ignorance I try to spare the same dense
Fault. By taking of you, I resolve on aim
For not making a useless step but to reclaim.
I am going in the path of the nature,
In expecting that it shows me this one of rapture.

VII

"I stand up on faith, on reason, to more charming
Delirium, without fear, without soul-searching.
Vicky told me, without the other misgiving
Than this one whose feeling of bliss is unremitting."

VIII

Am I going at this time to abridge a sweet
Fate? Am I going to trouble a pure and concrete
Heart? Ah, all the cost of life is in the proper
Felicity that we have to taste for ever.

IX

"Even by putting the roof to our bliss, I destroy
To it the greatest charm, she said; this supreme joy
Hundred times sweeter to hope that obtains it. For
We thus enjoy better when we expect it more
Than we taste it; let us live in the dream encore."

X

Angel Gabriel! Lend the pencil of bliss!
O divine angel Michael! Teach to my amiss
And rude pen to describethe enjoyments
Of the love and of the innocence; that enchants!

XI

"Hide your deceptive arts ahead the sainted truth
Of the nature. Have only the natural ruth,
The sensible heart, the honest soul; then let err
Your counstraintless imagination on proper
Transports of two youngspouses quite very tender
Who1, under the watch of their parents, indulge in
The sweet illusion that flatters them, she told, who2
In the ecstasy of desires slowly advance through
The end, interlace from flowers and from garlands
The happy bond that must unite us till the ends.

XII

So many charming pictures elates me, I put
Them together orderlessly. For great doubt
And the delirium that they cause me stop me
Binding them because we procure the few idea
About the comfort, about what is beautiful
And honest, and the unfairness of other troubleful

States makes these people see the binjustice in his
Vices. Indeed man who exactly passes
His whole life to work for living has no other
Idea than this of his work or his proper
Interest, and all his mind seem to be in his arms.

XIII

I am well-learned, well-formed of sprit and body,
Strong, sane, alert, robust, full of sense, of bounty,
Of reason, of humanity; I have custom,
Tastes; I love the beautiful; I do what is wisdom;
And I do what is right, sometimes what is wrong; free
From the empire of cruel passions, and scot-free
From the York of opinion, but submissive to
The rule of the wisdom, and docile to the true
Voice of the friendship. I possess all the useful
Talents and several agreeable and peaceful
Talents; I am worry a little about wealth, for
My resource is at my arm's length, I want to explore.

XV

"you are in ecstasy from a nascent passion,
Your heart is open to first flame of compassion,
To the first fire of love; your sweet illusions make
You a new universe of delices and of fake
Possessions. This the connection of heart,
This is the contest of honest feelings, show of art
That first penchant from. Do not unite persons who
Do not suit only in a given condition too,
And who will not suit anymore; this condition
Came to change, but persons who will suit in some position
They are, she said, in some chaos they enter, envision."

XVI

I expect by reminding you that I give you
A natural talent for governing me, too
You secure me to be contradictory on
The principles, you make mistake. There is quite
The difference between to assume the right
To command, and to govern the one who commands
The enterprise of a wife is certain reprimands
Or some empire of sweetness, certain manners
And certain complacencies and behaviors.
Her orders are like caresses, her threats are like
Tears. She has to reign in the house as an alike
Queen in the kingdom, this is everything I like.

XVII

So she told: "it is constant that the best lover
Is the one where the woman has the most power;
But when she spouses the voice of chief, she wants to
Usurp her sights and to command herself; and too
It never results of this trouble than misery,
Scandal and dishonor;that3 brings the poverty."

XVIII

It is difficult to find in the scum of earth
A spouse capable of making the normal mirth
Of a honest man: not as he is the most
Vicious in the last ranks than the first ranks almost.

XIX

"your heart is always the same, but your apropos
Opinions change. Your feelings, slower to undergo
A change for the worst. You risely raised, she told me,
In the house of your father in your countryside,
I examine at time that you arrive at the side
Of Manhattan, or you enter into the world.
Before you thought very well on honesty, pearled
Conduct, and you have the will also sane than theory;
You have scorn for vice and horror for debauchery."

XX

You always came back to the lessons of your own
Parents and of your teachers as a stiff jargon;
And the duties that they preached as a childish
Morals that we have to reject as the old wish.

XXI

"Do not run after the new idesa, you could not
Manage your brain. For I want to make you feel
All the ideas quite salutary and useful
To the man have been the first known, the most boastful.
This way of making you admire does not touch me,
You know where you have to find the felicity
Of your life and in what you can contribute
To joy of others, she told me, be resolute."

XXII

I thought hundred times with fight that if I had
The bad luck of occupying today such mad
Employ that I think, tomorrow I will be almost
Inevitably tyran, destructor the most
Harmful for my wife, enemy of equity,
And of all kind of virtues and of decency.

XXIII

"From this immense provision that covers our land,
I would find out what is agreeable and grand
For me, I can be better appropriate me.
The first usage of my wealth would be to put money
Into the spare time, she said, leizures and freedom."

XXIV

As you buy me with the temperance, and there is
No true enjoyment in the life without the breeze
Of health. I would stay near you, and it would be
Possible for flattering the senses that truly
I received from you. I am sure that the more you
Put yours in my possession, the more I find me too
In the reality. For the wealthy people,
Their great fails, this is the annoyance; in middle
Of many entertainments quite assembled little
At great prices, in the middle of so many
Persons who compete to please them, the ennui
Still cosumes them and kills them. They passed their life to
Escape it, but they never attained it. The few
Women specially who do not know how to care
Themselves either to enjoy themselves, are tired where
They are. That turns for them a horrible harm that
Sometimes takes off the reason, the vie format.

XXV

She said: "I do not know much about the frightful
  Than this one of a beautiful wife quite useful
Who suffers from bad conception of her husband,
Who still ties to him, who changes or does intend
  To change in idle wife; thi is my own demand."

XXVI

The proprieties, the vogues, the usages
  That are derived from good air and from luxuries
Confine the course of the life in the gloomy,
  Sullen and disappointing uniformity.

XXVII

"the ridicule, that the opinion redoubts on
  All facts, is always there for tyrannizing upon.
This is the only opinion that makes everything
Difficult, that chases bliss to us, she said, during."

XXVIII

It is not enough that the women
  Are estimable, they must be esteemed; again
  It is not enough for women to be pretty,
They must be please; it is not enough for them to be
Wise, they must be renown for such; their happiness
  Is not only in their conduct and politeness,
  But in their reputation; it is not possible
That the one who consents to pass for contemptible
  Or reprehensible can never be honest.
  It is good to observe the children so modest
Until the age where the treason and where nascent
Feeling makes conscience speak and take under advisement.

XXIX

"there is no veritable love without ardor,
And no enthusiasm without a matter
Or object of real or chimerical perfection,
But the love consists on the perception
Or daydream or imperfection, she then told me,
From what lovers will be inflamedfor whom this easy
Perfection is nothing more, who4 do not miss to
See in what they love than the object of sex too"

XXX

No, this is not thus that the soul becomes excited
And indulgence in its transpots that make the incited
Delirium of lovers and the charm of their
Passions. All are only illusions in the square
Love, I vow; but what is real, there are the feelings
That animate usfor the true and beautiful things
That makes us love. This beautiful thing is not in
The object that we love, it is the work of your thin
Mistakes. Who is the veritable lover who
Is not ready to immolate his true life to
Her life? Where the sensual passion in a man
Who knows the debauch and who wants die again?

XXXI

She said: "the true motives of delight always speak
In the heart of a wife of judgment so classic
Who tends to look for in her state the happiness
Of her life. The chasteners must be in goodness
Or in virtue quite delicious for a pretty
Woman who has some elevation so dainty
In the soul. She wins on all and herself forever;
She builds in her own heart a throne to which all men

Come to render homage; the sentiments often
Jealous or tender, but always respectful for
Both sex, the universal esteem and hers encore
Prosper, endlessy pay tribute of glory to
Her the combats of some instants quite very due.
The privations are fleeting, but the price is so
Permanent, what a pleasure for a soul also
Noble, and the pride of the virtue joins to beauty;
And when her beauty will be no more, her glory
And her leisures will remain forever. And we
Will enjoy the past.that does not naturally
Suit all men to feel what motive the love of honest
Conduct can give to the soul, and what a modest
Strength we can find in us when we desire to be
Virtuous. There are the husbands to whom really
All that is wonderful appears chimerical,
And who in their baseness and scatological
Or vile reason will never feel what the folly
Of virtue can haveon human passion really."

XXXII

By thinking about evething you say, I find
That all those arragements too premature are unkind
And misunderstood, and that it is abused to
Mean two children to unite with each other too
Before being able to know if this union
Is in the order of nature as communion;
If they would have between them the suitable
Connections for making this union viable.
Do not mix what is natural at the wild state,
And what is natural at the civil state.
In the first state, all the women fit all the men,
Because the ones and the others have only again
The primitive and common form; in the second

State, each character was developed and wakened
By the social institutions, and each received
Its proper and determined form, not only perceived
Education, but of well or ill orderly
Competition of the natural study.
Do you want to prevent the abuses and to
Make the happy marriage, suffocate the true
Prejudices, and forget the human tradition.

XXXIII

She told: "my passion is not cruel, it is pure
For the heart that experiences it; it is poor.
The honesty forms it, and the innocence too
Nourishes it. Happy husband! The charm of virtue
Only makes add the love for you, and the sweet link
That assits you is not less the price of your blank
Wisdom than this one of your attachment. All are
Good when you stay the master; all are so bizarre
And wrong when you let you go free with it. What is
Banned by nature, this is to extend our enemies
The most distand than our strength; what is forbidden
By the nature, this is to want what we cannot then
Obtain; what is banned for us by the conscience is not
To be attempted, but to let us win by a lot
Of temptation. Attachment does not depend on us
To have or not to have the passions, but it thus
Depends on us to reign on the passions. therefore
All feelings that legitimate to us, more
All those that dominate us are cruel. Encore,
A man is not guilty of loving the woman
Of another man, if he thinks very often
That this passion is miserable, abservient
To the policy of the duty quite lenient;
He is guilty of loving his proper wife at

A level of immolating all to his love pat.
Do not expect from me long precepts of morals;
I have only one to give you, that one assembles
All the others. Be man; pull your heart out of limits
Of your condition. Study and know these ambits;
Whatever narrow they are, you are not broken
As much as you confine yourself in it again.
You are miserable when useless desires. Whence
You put to rack of possible what is not, thence
You are despairing when you forget your duty
Of man for forging yourself as imaginary."

XXXIV

The only goods whose the privations costs are those
To which we believeto have right, as we expose.
The evident impossibility to obtain
It detaches from it. Illusions are the vain
Harms; but the contemplation of human heartbreak
Makes the sage always moderate and sometimes fake.
We are mortal and perishable, will we go
To form the eternal knot on this earth apropos
Where all change, where all pass, and whose I will disappear
Tomorrow. O Vicky, my wife! By losing you there,
What would it rest to me. Andneverthless I must
Learn to lose you. Do you want to live happy, just
And wise, tie to your heart only to the beauty
That does not die. Extend the law of necessity
To the moral things; learn from all to leave when virtue
Orders it, to put yourself above events, to
Detach your heart without the passions tear it,
To be bold in the adversity; to be licit
And firm in your duty, in order to never
Be animal. Then you will be happier
Despite the fortune, and wisw despite the passions.

Then you will find in the possession as fashion
Certain fragile goods a volupty that nothing
Can trouble; you will possess without possessing
You. And you will feel that the man, to whom all then
Escape, only enjoys from what he knows often
To lose. You will not have illusion of dreamy
And imaginary pleasures; you will not truly
Have the pains that are the fruits of it; you will gain
So much at this exchange; for those pains are so vain,
Frequent and real, and those pleasures are and rare;
Victorious on so many false and unfair
Opinions, you will be the one who gives a great
Price at the life. You will pass yours without the straight
Trouble and you will end it without fight; you will
Untie from it as all the matters. You will still
Know other glory than to be beneficent
And fair. I do not know the other enchantment
Than to live independent with what we love, by
Gaining all days of appetite and health by
Our works. All those embarrassment whose you really
Speak to me do not even normally touch me.

XXXV

She said: who knows where we can live freeborn5 and free
Withoiut having needed of harming anybody.

XXXVI

Believe me that the America is always
Permitted to be honest and fair, it does raise
Us with prestige and pride of finding our proper
Citizenship. We are sure of subsisting ever
Without intringue, whitout deal, without dependence,
This is to live with our jobs and good presence.

1-who, under the watch of their parents, indulge in, who being a relative pronoun of spouse is the subject of verb indulge. 2-who in the ecstasy of desires slowly advance, who being a relative pronoun of spouses is the subject of verbs advance and interlace.. 3-that brings the poverty, that being a demonstrative prnoun is the subject of verb brings. 4-who do not miss to se, who being a reltive pronoun of lovers is the subject of verb miss. 5-freeborn means independent.

No 74

Story of Tum with his wife

I

I recognize your heart at the glimmer of nice
Lanterns that cut as a lightning twilight. Precise
Exaltation slips out of this love that is most
Embalmed by passion across all, and that1 almost
Perfumes the atmosphere where you want to live. For
You have of words so affectuous and of looks more
Proud, of manners so diverse, I do not distinguish
The egoism of charity, either lavish
Corruption of virtue; all are seen by hawser2.
I have all the hurts of the world to conquer
Your scruple, and this is today that you even
Decide to accept me, o my charming lover!

II

"The beuty of this diamond makes for you
An admirable effect on yoiur spirit. Too,
You good bias for touching my heart so due.
You are joyful without perceiving the abyss
Where you rush at a level you married me. This
Is hard to say. It is the freshness of my beauty,
I have the stain of marriage and the early
Adulterous illusions; I coul even
Place my life on a great heart quite so solid, then
The virtue, the tenderness, the volupties and

The duty mix together; I am glad and grang."

III

I do not love all the hope, for there is for me
As a certain promise, balancing truly
In the furture; such a fruit of gold is hanging
On fantastic foliage. What are you thinking.

IV

She said: "That you offered me before wedding
Is an imagined lie for despair of craving.
All those erratic disparagements fade under
The poetry of role that invades me. Further,
I was taken toward the man by illusion
Of the personage. This is a disillusion."

V

I did not make mistake. You talked to me about
A Sonson. The souvenir of Sonson, without doubt,
Passed in your soul as a great lightning in a night
Quite somber. When I want to work, you are at flight.
You involved in the night as the indistinct
Lamentation of a vague distress; and through tinct
Ring of sleigh bells, the murmur of trees and the more
Of hollow box; you have something distant encore
That overthrows you.that one came down in bottom
Of your soul as a whirl in an abyss, seldom
Took away among the spaces of a sweet
Melancholy quite limitless or infinite.

V

"I enjoy this love by a discreet, absorbent
Manner, that3 trained me, she told, by all impudent4
Artifices of my tenderness. I shiver
That it does not lose later, I do not expect further."

VI

Where came from that insuffisance of life quite mean,
This staneous stain of matter where you lean
On. Each smile hides a yawn of ennui, each joy
A malediction in you, and look like a toy.
All best kisses left on your lips a sentimental
Desire of a higher volupty quite vital.

VII

She said: "I have this muddle of common matters
And I scarched where the vulgar custom and manners.
I believe to forsee the revelation
Of an excentric existence, the dislocation
Of feeling, and always a some scorn of social
Conventions. They are a pile of autochtonal
Ganaches in vest of flannel, and of religious
Rights to warmer foot and to chaplet that thus
Sing endlessy to my ears: ' the social must"; for
The must, this is to feel what is great, to adore
What is beautiful, and not to accept the whole
Conventions of the society, with the droll
Ignominy that they impose us as a role."

VIII

This is that conjuration of world irritates you.
The instincts the noblest, the sympathies quite due
And the purest are persecuted and
Denigrated by you; you even blame your godsend.

IX

She said: "Why do you make me cry? I cannot love you.
Let me go somewhere to find my rest quite so due.
Leave me right now, I want a new life, a lover too.
O Sonson! I am happy to come back to you."

X

"Why have we known each other? What fate wanted it?
This is, Sonson said, through remoteness as two infinite
Rivers that flow for meeting; our particular
Slopes push us one on other. Now my singular
Hands squeeze yours, I feelthem quite warm and trembling
As a captive turtledove that has in need of taking
Back its flight, but retained by my certain something."

XI

She said: "I do not come to see you, I adore
What surrounds you. Tonight, all the nights, I therefore
Got up, I arrived until you; I watched your nice
House, the roof that shines under the lights; precise
Trees of garden that say at your windows; a little
Light, a glimmer that shine through the tiles quite brittle.
Oh! you do not know that there is here, so near and
So distant, a forlorn poor that is put at an end."

XII

"You are in my soul as a green on a pedestal,
On a high, solide and immaculate circle.
I need you for living! I need your eyes, your vpoice
And your thoughts, Sonson told; be my friend, I rejoice!"

XIII

She said :" A silence is everywhere, something sweet more
Seems coming out of trees. I feel my heart encore,
Whose the beatings start again, and the blood truly
Flows in my veins as a river of milk quite free."

XIV

Sonson said: "I hear quite in distance, above the trees,
On the high hills, certain vague and prolonged screeches,
In those screeches, there is a voicethat dawdles, and
I listen quietly, that5 mingles with a grand
Murmur, that6 looks for the imaginary
Satisfactions for its personal lechery."

XV

"the imitation caused by your presence is enough
To make me happy. I possess, she said, this tough
And better passion that is held until then as
A remarkable bird to pink plumage that has
Its flight in the splendor of the poetic sky
You tell sweet words with a voice so shaking and shy."

XVI

"What I want fro ypou, this is not the vain favors,
This is the soul of your body, this is ardors
Of your age, this is the blood of your veins. And when

The noise of your steps remove, I believe again
That my heart stops beating. As soon as this step I
Expect and I love comes to hit my ears and I sigh,
Remind that I am alive and I feel that
My soul comes back. What a voice do you desire that
Is more loving? Sonson indeed replied like that."

XVII

"This is a noble intent, worthy of a faithful
Heart! She said: I smell perfume of your breath quite full
Of hope. Is not this that it is sweet to love and to feel
Loving each other, and that this is a real
And sweet thing to speak about love to each other
The night when everything is in rest and slumber.
With my husband Tum, the first month of marriage
Was honey moon, second month was an absinth quite liege."

XVIII

Ah! This would be a crime to let the flower fall!
Your soul always appears pure to me as your call
And your beauty. Sing for me some songs the night
You enchanted me, with the tears in your eyes quite!
I never had a heart more penetrated than
Yours, never a bush more ravishing that often
Expresses feelings more moving by those loving
Talkings of fire that the feelings are inspiring
The greatest welldoings and the transports the most
Tender of love the most legitimate almost.

XIX

She told: "I think that all laws were made for helping
The citizens as much as for intimidating
Them. My principal problem with Sonson is to

Distangle the truth that I try to mystify too.
Instead of wise reflections, my soul exalted
By those sounds so full, wanters in the invented
And imaginary spaces. A half- darkness,
A splendid freshness in it ; nevertheless,
I am so embalmed by the perfumed of dainty
Flowers. The silence, the deep solitude, the breezy
Freshness of long naves make the sweetest, nicest dream
Of Sonson. I love him a lot, that makes me scream.
But I have to go back to my husband so extreme."

XX

Tum said: "Have pity for me! You do not understand
What I suffer. My soul almost gives up its glistened
Mortal envelop. Don't forget you are a godsend."

 XXI

"The jealousy and calumny hunt you. Further,
In some place that providence puts you, your proper
Spouse will never see you without hating you; during
If I feign to love you, this will be for betraying
You. Your job is more important than my craving."

XXII

"To that, there is a remedy; I have only
Help of God. Let you be full of integrity
Or pure; and this is the only remedy that
I see for you. If you keep verily a pat
And invincible grasp for me, for everything
Will be changed soon or latter, Tum was then saying:"

XXIII

"In the words the most joyful and inappearance
The most peaceful. Ah! Great God! I see hell, she said, whence
What horrible punishments! I deserve them. Too,
I would like to stick to you as the ivy to
The rampart. You are a husband quite very due."

XXIV

Tum said: "you pursue to know what you justly hear
In the life by the words of felicity, cheer,
Passion and ecstasy that have appeared to you
So beautiful in the books and in the review.

XXV

"I am going to confession, I am going
To invent the little sins, so to be staying
For a longtime, to kneel in the shadow during.
The comparisons of finance, spouse, godly
Lovers and esternal marriage that truly
Come back in the sermon raise in the bottom
Of my soulcertain unexpected and random
Sweetness. The priest preached the respect that I owe
To the Saints, and to the Martyrs, and apropos
He gave me so many good and nice advices
For modesty of body, she said, and realease
Or salvation for the soul, I acted as horses
That they pull by the bridle. Those are my remorses."

XXVI

"You sweetly make drowsy at mystical langor
That exhale perfumes of altar, Tum said, or inner
Shrine, freshness of holy water and of radiance
Of wax candles; all express something to your presence".

XXVII

"A lover, in the contrary, should not all know,
Should not excel in of multiples apropos
Activities; and you should initiate you to
The energies of passion, she said, to the true
Refinements of the life, at all mysteries too."

XXVIII

"Your life is cold as an attic, Tum said, whose the dormer
Window is to north, and the ennui ever
Spins its web in the shadow at all corners
Of your heart. You know I forgive you; we are lovers.

XXIX

"In your indifferent looks float the inquietude
Of passions daily assuaged; and through your rude
Manners that particular brutality
That communicates the passions of things easy
In which strength practices, she said, where vanity
Gets amused. How the stars smile at you and me."

XXX

"The night is dark. Some drops of rain fall down. You thus
Breathe the damp breezethat refreshens your unctuous
Eyelids. The music of dance hums in your ear, and
You make some efforts for keeping you awakened,
In order to prolong the illusion or vapor
Of this pompous life, Tum said, that you surrender."

XXXI

"Sometimes the future lives in us without we know.
It, our words, she said, that we think we lie or we throw.
Off the scent draw a very next applicable.........5…
A vice so extendedis not condemnable."

XXXII

"Tum said: "New-York, vaster than ocean, sparkles to
Your eyes in a rosy atmosphere. For the true
Numerous life that stirs in that tumult have been then
However divided by listed parties in
Distinct scoreboard. As the morphinance turns morphine.
1-and that almost perfumes the atmosphere, that being relative
pronoun love is the subject of verb perfumes. 2-hawser means
cable. 3-that traied me, that being a relative pronoun of love is
the subject of verb trained. 4-impudent means extravagant in the
improper sense. 5-that mingles with a grand murumur, that being
a relative pronoun of voice is the subject of verb mingles. 6-that
looks for the imaginary, that being a relative pronoun of voice is
the subject of ver looks for. 7-the dots of suspension replce reality

No 75

Age of childwood

I

Alas! How many voices are going to raise
Against me? I have heard at a distance the blaze
Of clamors of this false wisdom that endlessly
Throws out of us, that always relentlessly pursues
A future that disappears as we advance with clues.
You answer me, my friend! The time of correcting
The bad inclinations of the human being
Is in the age of childwood where the pains are less
Tender for sparing them in the age of soudness.

II

My dear comrades, who told you that all this order
Is now at the disposition of the youngster,
And all this nice instructions that the teacher heaps on
The weak mind of a child will not be on day more fun
Or more pernicious than useful? I look upon.
O teachers! Who garanteesyou that you spre something
By grieves thatyou lavish on the naïve youngling.
O professor! Why do you give him more malaise
That his state does not have it and does not raise.

III

Without being sure that these present malaises
Are at the charge of future? And how will you seize
Or will you prove me that these bad penchats whose you
Pretend to heal them just come to the child so due
From your dubitious and quite misunderstanding
Cares more than the nature and than the course of thing?
Poor foresight on the hope quite well or ill-founded
To make him happyt one day, that makes him1 wounded
As if those vulgar reasoners mix the licence
With the freedom, and the child that the people sense
To make happy with the child that people make worst;
Let us learn them todistinguish both at first.

IV

For not running after the chimeras, may us
Not forget what suits our condition or status.
The humanity has their place in the order
Of things; the child has his in the human life, yonder.
To assign everyone to his place and to fix it
To him, to order the human passions quite discrete
According to constitution of man is all
That can do for his well-being or his call.

V

The rest depends on the diverse causes that are
Not in our power. Whence we do not know so far
What is the happiness or the misfortune
Absolute. Everything is mixed in the jejune2
Life; we do not taste about it no pure feeling.
Affections of our souls, as modifications
Of our bodies, are in of endless mutations.
The good and the bad are common to the other

People and to us, but in different metter3.
1-that makes him wounded, thatbeing a relative pronoun pf
foresight is the subject of ver makes. 1-that makes him, him
replaces child. 2-jejune means ordinary. 3-metter means measure

No 76

Excess of desires

I

For the happiest is the one who keeps his chin1
Up and the least pains; the miserable is often
The ones who feels the least pleasure in his existence.
The felicity of man on-earth is only
A negative state, we have to size it truly
By slightes lot of harms that we take patiently.
Listen to me! All feelings of pain are really
Attached with the desire of freeing totally
Itself from it. All ideas of pleasure are then
Attached with desire of enjoying it often.

II

All desires suppose the privations, and all
Privations2 that we feel are painful, tend to fall
Us. This is the disposition of our desires
And our faculties that consist our great dires3.
A tender- hearted guy whose the faculties would
Equal the desires would be quite happy and good.
In what does consist the path of properity
Or the human wisdom? This is not precisely
To reduce our desires; whence if they were abobve
Our power, a part of our faculties or of
Our abilities would remain doing nothing,
And we will not delight in all our being.

This is not either to broaden our faculties.
Whence if our desires at the same time increase
In greater rapport, we will become only dire4:
But this is to reduce the excess of desire5
On our faculties, and to put in real and leal
Equality the influence and the good will.
This is only when all the force is in motion
That the soul remains calm, that man in his caution
Is well-organized and complete in the action.

IV

The nature quickly shows the man that the desires
Are necessary and the faculty inspires
The enough for satisfying them. It bhas put
All others in reserve at its bosom so brute
For spreading them to the need quite so umoot6
The man is often less miserable when he
Is in the privation of all. The misery
Does not consist in the privations of the things,
But in the need that is felt; these are our carkings7.

V

The real world has its bounds and imaginary
World is infinite. Whence this is their only
Difference that all the distresses that truly
Make us miserable arise naturally.
If we remove wealth, health, good testimony
Of self; all distinctions of this life are not really
In the opinion. Of course, if we remove pains
Of body and remorses of the conscience, chains
Of humiliation; all our hurts are truly
Dreamy and without bounds of possibility.

VI

The man is very strong whe he is so content
Of who he is. He is very impuissant
When he wants to rise above the humanity.
Do not imagine you only in the broadening
Your faculties, but what is important is making
The most of you. You reduce them in the other
Hand,if your pride extends more than them. And measure
The ray of our sphere, and let us stay to center
As spider in the middle of its webs, yonder.

VII

All animals have exactly necessary
Abilities for protecting themselves; only
Man has the non-essentials. Is not it quite strange
That the superfluous is tool of our derange8?
Often the better way of giving stuffs to us
Whose we lack is to remove thes ones that we thus
Have. This is by dint of working onour delight,
We will alter it in misery or in plight9.

VIII

It is hard to die, without doubt; but it is sweet
To live everyday in a hope quite incomplete.
What resource, what hope, what consolation would it
Leave to us against the rigors of the bit
Of fate and against injustices illicit10.

IX

There are only the half-knoledge and false wisdom
That invent the worst of harms to us at random.
The need of dying is only a reason to
Wise man for supporting the pains of the life too.

X

Wise man knows to stay at his place, but man-child who
Does not know his cannot hold it and stays untrue.
Man-child is submitted to others because of
His necessities, and because he sees above
All what is useful to him, and what is able
To provide or to brother his exchange verbal11.

XI

And on-earth, there are two kinds of depedences:
This one of things of lumps of matters that12 is
The nature, this one of men that is society.
The dependence of things has no morality
And does not bother freedom of communities,
Does not producein middle of us vices.

XII

Dependence of men being confused engenders
All the vices; this is by it that the masters
And subordinates are depraved mutually
Or throw themselves in the dense immorality.

XIII

If certain measure really supposes to be
Taken about the harm in the society,
Tis is to substitute the laws for the people,
To arm the general wills with a principal
Force quite very superior to the action
Of particular will, to will of a fraction.

XIV

The laws of United Nations were able to
Inflexibility that no human influence
Is unable to defeat. Whence the dependence
Of menjust becomes this one of things, I advance.
1-keeps his chin is locution that means suffers in the improper
sense. 2-privations is the subject of verb tend. 3-dires uses as
a common noun and means miseries and woes. 4-dire means
miserable.. 5-desire is written at the singular because of the rhyme.
6-umoot means having a particular signification. 7-carkings
means worries.and miseries.. 8-derange uses as a common noun
and means foolishness. 9-plight means complication. 10-illucit =
illicit injustices. 11-verbal = exchange verbal. 12-that is the nature,
that being a relative pronoun of of one is the subject of verb is.
13-dependence is the subject of verbs has, bother, produce.

No 77

Switching to democrat

I

Vicky, by seeing you so sensitive and so
Beautiful, could you not to believe apropos
To the democrat party, to you it sends hello.

II

How you reveal me your heart, this treasure so full
Of ineffable kindness! Close to your peaceful
Reside where humanity bemoans and pines,
Accept to arrange you in the democrat lines.

III

According to Vicky, the democrats send me
To represent the angels of hope. Normally,
The religion accuses us too much liberal.
As if I rejectedexcellent and vital qualities
Qualities of their hearts that so many human
Beings or followers love in principle then.

IV

It1 could neverthlessaccuse the democrats
Of making you forget God, the sky, the combats.
Vicky, my daughter! They are making you contemplate
The heart, the soul, the happiness and the life so straight

By contemplating ahead your bounties, your strong......2
It is not God, cannot judge what is right and wrong.

V

I understand quite well the veritable love
Excludes baseness, the fraud, the hypocrisy of
So-called leaders, and inhumanity;
And they ally themselves more to the sympathy;
They never stop spurring and formenting, unless
They ask grace for themselves or for their weakness.
They said: "You must forgive our licences in such
Diversions that bring no damage to our much
Pains, in compensation of bile whose we have drank much.
It could nevertheless accuse, it replaces religion.
2-the dots of suspension replace state.

No 78

Star of love

I

The hand that hangs in the space has only written
A strong word in letter of fire. Both lovers then
Live because they move, and the sun would fall in dust,
If one between them stpped loving. Life and love just
Are an only act for Efept. What a malice,
At the same time what a tenderness! What a peace!
The bush smiles and the eyes shine, glossy by the quick
Emotion. The scene of love under the trees does pick
A sweet sensitivity, a honest and pure
Passion ravishing1; some kisses that makes them sure.

II

Remind the night so pure during which Efept and
Odette met under the trees of park very grand;
As them, pay attention: "This is the voice of night,
This is the warble of the birds that then invite
To the happiness." With them, contemplate Venus:
The star of love, the most beautiful and precious
Pearl of the ocean of nights." Do you envisage
As Efept that2 the stars love each other and presage
On each other, that3 the moon takes form for kissing
The ocean, that4 the forests and rocks are going
To speak; and you do not feel a little distant
For world of shakespeerian fairy event5.

III

Ah! Precisely, the longest patience and stronger
Obstination must thus, the one and the other,
End sooner and later. What one brooks will become
Incurable what one does not cure with wisdom.
What worries me when you are vexed, this make you glide
Some vulgar words. Without knowing, you turn aside
The flower of the politeness that specially
Distinguishes you; and this is the modesty.
1-passion ravishing = passion that ravishes. 2-that the stars love
each other, that being a conjunctive pronoun is the complement
of direct object of vern envisage. 4-that the moon takes form,
that being a conjunctive pronoun is the complement of direct
object of verb envisage.. 4-that the forests and rocks, that
being a conjunctive pronoun is the complement of direct
object of verb envisage. 5-event means scene, stage setting.

No 79

Conscience and passion

I

O gods of earth! You wish to break the links that then
Bothers you. You tire me with your plaints; so often
You reproach me about my comportment so due
When I am the most tender occupied by you.
By wanting to see you glad, I make you angry.
O my brother in Christ, I will never agree
To bear the pain of being odious to you.
Your joy is so costly than the worthy price too.
Being by obeying me, and then ask me count
Of my orders; I will be ready to recount
You the reason soon as you will be in the state
Of listening me; I will never consternate
To take you for judge between you and me. My brother,
Jesus-Christ can change your mind and makes you better.

II

Those who want to guide wisely the youths for protecting
Them from the traps of senses are pertubating
Them about the love and crime and would do a crime
To them. All deceptful ideas that the sublime
Heart denies do not persuade. The young people
Driven by an instinct smile at the biblical
Maxims to which they feign to agree and only
Wait the moment of making them or empty.

I will never fear to cultivate in the men
The fine feelings whose they are eager; I even
Draw them to them as the permanent happiness
Of life because they are real; this is not a guess.

III

By adjusting the good sentiments in the men,
I want that they carry them out; so often,
By making them feel what charm adds to the appeal
Of senses the union of heart. Really, I will
Disgust them in the libertinage; I will make
Them wise in making them loving as a sweet cake.
The conscience is the voice of the soul; the passion
Is the voice of the flesh. The reason in fashion
Deceives us so often; but the conscience never
Deceives, it is the true guide of man forever.
Whence the acts of the conscience are not of judgments,
But of sentiments. Although all the vast contents
Of our ideas come to us from outside; feelings
That appreciate them are outside of our beings.

IV

And this is by them1 only that we know again
The convenance and disconvenance that often
Exist between us and the things that we have to
Respect or to avoid. In us these things are true.
The conscience is at the soul what the instinct is
To the body; the one who follows it agrees
Or obeys to the dense nature and does not fear
To lose his way; for him nothing appears so dear.
The modern philosopher, who only admits
What the conscience explains, naturally permits
Or accepts this obscure faculty called "instinci"

That appears to guide the animals so distinct
Through some purpose without acquired knowledge, without
Discernment on the existence of God, no doubt.

V

The instinct, according to the one of our wise
Philosopher (Condillac), is only a guise
Of custom deprived by the reflexion, and then
Acquired by thinking or meditating often.
Conscience! Conscience! Divine instinct! Immortal and
Celestial voice! Guide very sure for an unbland
Being very limited, but intelligent
And free! Unfalling judge quite very permanent
Of good and of evil, who especially
Makes the man similar to God very Holy.

VI

O conscience! This is you that makes the excellence
Of the nature of human hearts, the temperance
And the morality of their actions; without
You I feel in me nothing that thus peeps me out
Above the animals that the sad privilege
Of wandering from mistakes by mistakes with bridge2
Of a nice understanding without rule, and then
Of a reason without principle again.
The virtue is opposite of vanity;
Honesty is popposite of laxaity2.

VII

I believe that the world is governed by a will
So mighty; I see it, or it I instead feel3
As this meeting becomes more interesting, I will
Try hard to win it until I shun all unreal

And idle questions that may embarrass or scate
My self-esteem, but that are useless to my faith.
Complaining that God lets the man do the evil,
    This is really complaining that he did revel
        To create human being with an excellent
Nature because he has just put to his constant
Actions the morality that ennobles them, and
Because he gives the virtue to him and free hand.
Supreme enjoyment is in the self-consentment,
    This is for deserving it that God pleases to plant
Us on the earth and we are due to the freedom
That we are then tempted by the temper-tantrum
    Or by the passions and definitely held back
By the conscience. The conscience is our true track.

VIII

What could the divine power do in our favor
,more? Could it put contradiction in our humor4
And give the price of having well made to dose whose
Have no power of doing bad, we have a clue?
For stopping the man being evil, may you try
To limit him to instinct and to make him shy
    And stupid? No, o God my soul, I never
Reproach you to have created him to your tender
Picture so that I may be free, good, and happy
As you; you teach me not to judge anybody.

IX

This is misuse of our faculties that makes us
    Miserable and evil. Our wrries, thus
Our problems, ourts come by ourselves. The moral
    Harm is incontestably our work; physical
Harm would be nothing without our vices that make

It sensitive to us and that render us fake.
Is not this for conserving us that the nature
Makes feel our needs? Are not the pains of structure
Corporal a signal that the machine breaks down,
And a warning to look for it. Do not crown,
Pride and vanity empoison your lives and ours?
Does God desire that we suffer at all the hours.

X

If we wre content of whom we are, we would not
Get to deplore our lot, but to look for a lot
Of imaninary comfort, we tend to give
Us thousand severe harms; that makes very active.
The one who cannot bear a little suffering
May expect to suffer a lot in his long-standing.
When we spoiled our constitution by disordered
Life,we want to restore it by the cures quite bettered.
My brothers, do not pursue the authoirs of harms;
Thse authors are yourselves. And there is no alarm
of harm than this one you do or you then suffer.
Each other has been in ourselves as improper.

XI

The general harm cannot be in the disorder
And I see in the system of world and order
That does not deny itself. The particular
People who suffer. The man did not receive it
From nature that is having so much clemency.
We have to follow impulsion of the nature;
We resist with it; by listening what feature
It told to our senses, we give a cold shoulder.
To what it revealed to our hearts quite so harder.
1-With bridge means with help. 2- laxity means corruption.
3-instead it I feel = I feel it instead. 4-humor means nature.

No 80

Tam is really in love

I

No man has only known himself, if even though
Someone knows himself and this is not quite so
Enough or adequate for making a judgment
Either about his species or about his descent
Or about the class that he ordinarily
Holds in the moral and social category1.

II

Many men, it is true, think of knowing others;
But they make mistake according to their brain-powers.
That is why it is so necessary to think
About it by the judgments that they just misthink.
Whence from all diverse judgments made by the guys
So skillful I know in my knowledge or my eyes
That there is nothing and even one has not been
Fair and in accordance to truth so genuine.

III

Instead of judging others by self without
Stopping at the pretty appearance, without doubt
It is necessary of judging self by others.
Meanwhile each believes to know himself, and his own
Individual is very often this one

That he knows less. If I were like this guy, I would
Do differently that he does not makes as good.

IV

Tum said:" I ignored that in eying Tyra
Hungrily she just saw me in a mirror, ah,
To wich I did not remind. Dhe came back and
Surprised me by a great rapture that made me grand
And that made me breathe out by stretching my both hands
Through her as at least we took a walk on the sands."

V

"You can imagine nothing equal to sudden
Terror whose I was amazed by seeing me then
Discovered in this attitude. She reassured
Me by looking at me with an eye enough insured.
In her full tenderness she showed me a better
Seat that we had access to conserve together."

VI

This were as one sees a declaration very
Ambiguous on both sides; and it seemed really
That nothing should lack between your friendshid
Of both beaus thus declared. Tum, your love seems so deep.

VII

"Guys, understand me! By idolizing her,
I found myself in the delicious and tender
Situation it is true, but under the most
Duress where I have been in my life. I almost
Dared neither to breath nor to raise the eyes; and then
If I had temerity of resting again

My hand on her knew, that would do so tenderly
That I believed that she did not feel it quickly."

VIII

"About my acquaintance with her, she did not talk
To me and did not look at me and did not walk
Near me. She and medid not make the least movement;
A profound silence established between my bent
And my feeling so hesitating, but the heart
Told and felt sensuation and thing apart."

IX

"She has modesty and sense of propriety.
She likes to talk about the virtue; honesty
Is the most important for her than life. And then
I could not tell how everything she made often
Appeared more impressive and more tender toi me.
This was what has compelled me to flirt heer daily."

X

If in this situation the both eyes met each
Other once, it is a good bye. I cannot reach
Her anymore, and the effect of glances that
Dashed toward the two eyes learned one another what
Dangers when one has been alone together. Whence
You have to put in application thc prudence.

XI

"It seems that she trats me as a thing that belongs
To her, she received in propriety as dongs.
The word of love has not been even told between
Us. But it is impossible of losing keen

Persuasion of having been passionately
Loved by her. She really warm my head so pretty."

XII

"Once, alas! Once in my life, my bush met hers, oh!
O souvenir! Will I lose you in the barrow?
Praise as long as it will please her with her obscene
Pleasures! I challenge you as long as she has been
To have tasyted something similar to the quick
Delice whose my heart was overcome for one week..

XIII

Alas, my God! I found in these kisses something
Sweeter and more impressive too and my trembling
Heart always more tendertended to fly ahead
Of acknowledgment of her friendship quite so well-bred.

XIV

Whence she remained immobile. That was natural,
By what was not true; and it appeared a normal
Glance that accompanied that silence and I will
Never forget it my life. And then this unreal
And imperceptible movement has eemed to turn
Away your gentle and faithful heart quite so stern.

XV

Her lips could resist to mine, and her pretty
Bush avoided all the kisses that she intends
To give to another. I feel that our love tends
Through the truth or the love of truth comes to be
The dearest because it costs me a lot. Ah! Whence
It is now my main passion and my reference.

XVI

This is the noblest virtue that can penetrate
In the heart of man and it is made for my state.
In all cabins, I heard murmuring at half-voice
The charming and delicious words that came to rejoice
Me; and I notice quite distinctly in this one
Of king a stir that did not augur badly like fun.

No 81

Canon of truth

I

I would like that the details of my life are known
By someone who loves the justice and the canon
Of truth and who are actuallky enough young.
For task to naturally follow me, but strong.
Therefore, after many long uncertainties, i
Then determine yourself to emit some high
Secrets of your heart in the little number,
But chosen by good guys who listen me yonder.

II

My enthusiasm made these measures very
Inadequate, and there is no other trusty
Method for protecting my trust than to place it
In the virtuous hearts quite honest and concrete
That can conserve this memory. It would be
Important for judging my conduct honestly,
Of knowing my temperament, my natural,
My character that by a clearness1 quite normal
Do not resemble to those of other men, by
Persisting in judging all my motives by.

336

III

In such case, those who judge by the appearances
Always deceive themselves and lose their natural senses.
Whence I confine myself to make you the faithful
Narrator of all that happened to my brimful
Heart. I want to remember you to listen me
With a worthy attention, not of the only
Importance of things that I get to tell you and
That2 by themselves do not deserve it3 or demand
It4, but of the job whose I dare to charge you out,
Job the noblest that man can then carry out
On thgeearth for all the prosperity. And then
If my name that has to live must pass again
With the opprobrium or with glory often.

IV

In this austere and sublime job, this is really
To the heart to purify the ears normally.
For me, I put myself in the necessity
Of accomplishing faithfully and entirely
Mine that is not always so fidele and so true,
But one more time to convince the shame and to
Scarify it to the verity quite so due.

V

Indeed, this will never be voluntarily
That I will commit such mistakes; I normally
Know that impartiality in a broadcaster
Only serves to him to make enemies for ever
Of each of them enough good for telling him
Neither enough bad for his colleagues so prim.

VI

This is for that motive I want to remain still
Unknown; my great excess is to impose my will
To only consult the reason and to only
Say the truth, so that according to the degree
Of my enlightments and the positions of my
Mind we will be able to find in me quite high
Sometimes a critic who pleases a jokes so often,
Sometimes a severe and surly sensor even.

VII

We are born weak, we need strength. We are born lacking
In all, we need assistance. we are born unthinking,
We need judgment. Wwe are born naïve or stupid,
We need understanding; we have to be lucid.
According to my intellectualknoledge,
Everything we do not habve greatly as the pledge
In our minds and everything we need in ourselves
Were given to us by education or booksheles.

VIII

Truly, this education comes from the nature,
Or from men or from things. The inside and mature
Development of our faculties or feature
And of our organs is education of nature.
The acquisition of our own experience
On the objects that thus affect us or our sense
Is the education of things. That's reference.
This development is schooling of men, no doubt.

IX

There are customs that they are only tense by force
That never suffocates the nature5 in its course.
Such is, for exemple, custom of plant whose they
Embarrass the vertical direction or way.
The plant becomes free and keeps the inclination
That they compelled it to take, no consideration.
The seed has no changed for that its ingenerate
Direction. And if the plant continues to vegetate,
Its deployment becomes again vertical. Then
It is the same for the inclinations of men.

X

As long as we stay in the same state, we can keep
The inclinatioins of the customs being deep
And the least natural to us. My dear crony6,
And as soon as the situations has only
Changed, the habitude begins by stopping daily
And the natural then comes back very quickly.
Since the antiquity, the education is
Certainly a custom. Are not there some bodies
Who forget and thus lose their own education,
And others who keep mit with consideration.

XI

We are born tender-hearted, and from our birth we
Are affected from diverse ways by the daily
Objects that encircle us. Soon as we again
Havethe conscience of our sensations. Soon as then
Disposed to search for or to truly run away
From objects that produce them following that they
Are agreeable or pleasant to us, and whence

According to convenance or disconvenance
That we find between us and those objects.

XII

our sensations being constraint by our custom
Become truly spoiled by our opinion seldom.
Forced to contest the social institution or
The nature, we special need to choose encore
Between making a man or a citizen; ever
We cannot do at the same time one another.
All pratical society, when it is narrow
And well-united, keeps away from blow-by-blow.
The essential is to beattentively good
With who we live, even if we are often rude.

XIII

In the social order, the one who in rapture
Tries to keep primauty of feelings of the nature
Does not know what he wants. Always in confusion
With himself, always floating between his function
And his penchant; nevertheless, it will never
Be also good either for him or for other.
For being something now, for being yourself and
Always one, we must act like we speak, like we command.
We must be always decided on the party
That you must take, follow it and to takeit highly.

XIV

I expect that they show us this prodigy for
Knowing if he is a man or citizen. More
When they want to send back to the chimerical
Town,they call institution of Platon, the total
PLatononly purified the heart of the man;

But Lyangue has just disorted it by its plan.
We start by the mothers, I will be surprised by
Certain changes that I produce or i supply.
Everything derives successively from that first
Depravation: all moral orders become worst;
The natural disappears in all the hearts.
The inside of the house takes an air less living;
The spectacle that thus affects a burgeoning
Family does not attach reat value quite bland.

XV

The habit does not strengthen bonds of blood. There are
Neither mothers nor fathers nor children so far,
Neither sisters nor brothers; all hardly meet each
Other; how would they love each other truly? Each
Only remembers oneself. Where the house is only
A sad solitude, it is so necessary
Of cheering up somewhere else or of making happy.
The attractions of domestic life is the best
Counterpoison of bad practices. The biggest
Worry of children, whose we believe to harden,
Become attractive; it makes father and mother
The most necessary, dearest on another;
It tightensbetween them the conjugal binder.

XVI

When the family is alive and animate,
The domestic cares make the dearest and so great
Occupation of the woman and the most so
Agreeable amusement of husband, I vow.
Once woman become again mothers, and soon
Men become fathers and husbands, again I tune.
Man who cannot complete the duties of father

Has no right of becoming it. I tell whoever
Has the entrails and neglects the sublime duties
That he will gainfor longtime bitter ditresses
On his fault, will never be consoled with worries.

XVII

How does it happen at a father of family
Of leaving his children to the apostasy7?
He pays another man for filling those happy
Cares that are at charge to him. O mercenary
Soul! Do you believe to give to you nice children
Another father with money? Do not you then
Make mistake about it; this is not even
A dad you give to your kids, this is a maidman.
We are born capable of learning; whence we know
Nothing about ourselves. The soul who is so
Chained up in some imperfect and half-formed organs
Has no feeling of his own existence or spans8.

XVIII

The movements and the cries of the baby who saw
The day are effects purely spiritless and raw,
Lacking in knowledge and in will. Nevertheless,
Let us suppose that a child hadin his birth
The statue and the strength of a made man in mirth
That he was born quite well-equipped in the bosom
Of his mother as Pallas came from the wisdom
Or brain of Jupiter. This man-child would be
A pure moron9, a puppet, a stationary10
Statue and almost insensitive. He would see
Nothing; he listened nothing; he knows no body.

XIX

The man-child cannot find eyes through what he would not need
To see; not only he perceived no fake or valid
Object out of him, he would not bring anything
In the organ of sense that makes him be seeing..........10.
The colors would not be in his eyes; sounds would not
Be in his ears; bodies that he touches a lot
Would not be on his, he could not arrive to gain
One of them; contact of his hand would be in his brain;
Indeed, all these sensations would join together
In one point; he only would live in the proper
Common sensorium; he has only one idea:
This one of mein which he brings all his funny
Feelings, his sensations and his pruriency.

XX

This idea or this feeling would be the only
Thing that he would have more than a household11 baby12.
This man-child being suddenly formed could neither
Stand up straight on his feet, whence he needs much longer
For learning to support himself in balance further.
Perhaps would he make the try, and you would ever
See this big and robust body truly remaining
Immobile as a rock, or crawling and dragging
Himself as a young beast or as a poor small thing.
He would feel the malaise of needs without knowing
Them, and without then imaginary anything
Of providing for it. There is no prompt touch in
Middle of muscles of gut13 and these ones of arms, legs, chin.

XXI

Malaise of needs expresses itself by signs when
The help of other is needed to fill it then.
How do you think of this brutal education
That sacrfices the present for a vocation
Of unsure future, that chrges a child of malaise
Of a kind and begins by making him all days
Woeful, in preparing for him a happiness
Whose I do not know what pretended joyfulness
That he is to believe and that he will never
Enjoy, gladness that father tends to embroider.

XXII

When I think that this teaching is reasonable
In its object, how we can see without normal
Indignation the poor ghildren submitted to
A yoke quite unbearable and condemned too
By continual jobs, jobs that coulkd not answer
A rent of seven hundred dollars and other
Needs quite necessary. Those poor children do pay
Every week for this nice happiness, what to say;
Without being assured that so many cares will
Never be useful to them! The age of the real
Happiness passes among tears, the corporal
Punishments, menaces of debts so terrible.

XXIII

Alas! Who really knows how many children die
Victims of the pride or the arrogance or the high
Extravagance of a father or a master?
Quite very happy of escaping for ever
From the cruelty, the only profit that they
Then pull from the afflictions is to die one day

Without regretting the life. Father, be human!
Nevertheless this is your first duty. you will
Be human for all states, for all the ages, still
For all that is not strange to man. What sagacy
Is there for you out of the whole humanity.

XXIV

Who from you sometimes has never worried this age
Where the rose is always on the lips, and the sage
Or soul is still in peace? Father, why do you like
To take off from little innocents quite childlike
The enjoyment of a time so short andcheerlike;
And of a happiness so precious whose they could
Not abuse? Why do you14 want to fill with the rude
Bitterness and with the pains the first rapid years
That will not come back for them, either for our spheres.

XXV

O father, do you know the time where the death waits
Your children? Do not prepare the regrets or freights
To you in taking off the little bit of time
That the nature gives them; soon they can feel sublime
Pleasure of being, see how they can enjoy it.
Make yourselself calm at some hours that God will admit
To call them, they will not go to their resting place
Without having tasted the life in a short space.

1-clearness means simplicity. 2-that by themselves do not deserve it,
that being a conjunctive pronoun is the complement of direct object
of verb get. 3- donot deserved it,it replaces attention.. 4- or demand
it, it replacesattention.5- nature is the subject of verb suffocates..
6crony mens friend. 7-apostasy means abandonment. 8-spans means
times. 9- moron means imbecile in the improper sense. 9- stationary
means immobile. 10-the dots of suspension replces it. 12-household
means ordinary in the improper sense. 12- baby means child.+

No 82

Opinion, religion and freedom

I

Certain persons have said that the morality
In the faculty of the knowledge of human
Behavior is a rash convention. For me,
The other objection is the following scan:
"The reason that thinks gets lost in the gainsaying2."
The defects of all system only consists then
On what the thinking reason tries to be catching3
The infinite, by arriving to use again
The finished categories,
Makes the infinite finite.
The reason with the stories
Can apprehend infinite
In a general way. Whence the contradiction
Is generated by the thought; and however,
It is important to notice or to mention
That the corresponding contradictions ever
In the democracy; also everywhere,
They4 thus launch forth in all trhe representations
Of the men. Whence those men have no conscience; and there
They have no modesty, but the confutations6.

II

People take conscience in the contradictions then
Produced7 by the thought and that the exclusive thought
Can resolve.proof having nevertheless gotten
Out from experience consists on having taught
That diverse ideas about democracy
Contradict themselves. This image of multiple
Forms of freedom that8 contradict themselves only
Is the depthless representation of vital
Stories of democracy
And we foolishly use it,
This difference specially
For dishonoring the fit
Freedom. When one is content with the idea
Of several forms of the freedom, one admits then
That there is a truthand one deduces that key9.
Truth of democracy may be so often
The opinions of thinkers. The opinion
Is contingent thought. A conception that is
Mine there is nothing universal. Try to seize:
A wild10 democracy is not fine in union.

III

If we hold11 this idea, we may not deny
Doubtlessly that the storyof the natural
Freedom does not essentially contain the high
Corruptions of the men and of the actual
World, and it12 does not present them to us under
Of the multiple forms. But this conception means
That those are the opinions that the earlier
Story of the freedom makes us know and parvenes
To us. Whence no country might
Bring its same democracy

To another country. Right,
What is opposed to only
Opinion, this is the truth. In its presence,
The opinion turns palic, or this is in front
Of truth that those that search opinionsin the dense14
Story and in the fact, truly pretend to want
Or to only find the opinions. We find there
Two antagonists that combat the false freedom.
Longtime ago this was opinion everywhere
That declared te impotence to the true wisdom;

IV

This was the opinion that has truly declared
The impotence to the reason or to the truth
Of knowing the true. Religions have often dared
To tell that for arriving at the truth; forsooth15,
One must avoid the reason and that the reason
Must low down ahead authority of the faith.
The religions continue, in their full season,
To tell that the reason protests against the rathe16
Virtue or morality,
The religious teachings and
Pious thoughts, that it17 only
Tries to render all the grand
Religious atheistic. In fact, according
To some philosophers the reason, the wisdom
And the particular conviction are needing18
To originate19 in the human being some
Obligations to recognize20 a true as true.
Any type of religions really tends to start
In virtue of the thinking opinion quite due.
The reason and freedom for it21 are as a dart.

V

Religion22 will turn later against itself and
Come to be the adversary of the self-will
And reason of the sake of faith and does not pretend
Only that the presentiment, the love, the skill,
Self-conviction, these subjectives elements are
The measure of what supposes to have the first
Worth of the man. This subjective so far
May achive in the opinions as nothing worst.
Whence the religion has made
From opinion, what must be
For the man, just a parade,
What is fundamentally
The affirmation of the faith and piety
That the reason cannot attain the truth. Often
The entire culture of the epoch has freely
Taken as principle that the true cannot then
Meet. This is a principle that one may ponder
As a signal23 character of epoch. Therefore
It24 happens in theology that one never
Looks for the true in the doctrine, in the folklore,

VI

In the religion, in the community. And
This is not a symbol: a confession of faith
That becomes the base that each person will pretend
To make for himelf according to his rathe25
And proper conviction. The theological
Sciences are naturally cultivated
In the point of view ethical and social;
This is what makes its beauties so elevated.
Naturally, one confines
Oneself to some storical

Researches in all the lines
As if there is nothing total
To do, but to know the different opinipons.
For in this case it26 is matter of the faith,
Those are subjective consideratioins, clarions27.
The development of the religios and smooth
Dogma is takenas a blend28 of confluent
Opinions so that the truth is not the purpose.
This opposition, between opinion or slant29
And truth, that is so remarkable and morose,

VII

And that is in full flowering of our time and
Very pronounced that we observe in the story
Of religion. Therefore we may not then demand
Either attain more what the religion really
Cannot give; we may not search in it29 a thoughtful
Satisfaction that may not not be supplied even
By a knowledge more developed. All doctrineful30
Opinion30, absolutely because they often
Display a particular
Level of evolution,
Depends on its regular
Era or generation,
And has been specially confined in its limits.
This individual is the son of his wont32
People, of his class and of the current of wits33,
He can redress himself as long as he will want;
For he belong to the unique and natural
Spirit that specially constitutes his substance,
His essence and his development quite normal;
There is nothing to see with a force of presence.

VIII

Now if, relatively to the diverse stories
Of religion, we thus start from this idea
That we cannot know the truth; the thinking senses
Have only produced the opinions; the dainty
Signification of the religion is more
Simple; this is the knowledge or unique science
Of great opinions; this is to say just by lore34,
Particularities of persons quite quick-sense.
Since the opinion is what
Is mine, it belongs to me;
Each one has his. About that,
Nothing is truly wordly.
What we just want to find in the religion and
In the fair freedom, this notion that already
Constitutes its interior and its so grand
Determination and the root of its only
Existence, taken38 as object for the thought. Thus
What the stories of the religion and freedom
Present to us, those are the acts of the precious
And thinking opinions that implant as wisdom.

1-scan means observation, examination. 2-gainsaying means
contradiction. 3-catching means apprehending. 4-they launch for,
they replaces contradictions. 5-they have no modesty, they replaces
men. 6-confutations means contradictions. 7-produced is an adjective
passed participle of contradictions. 8-that being being a relative
pronoun of forms is the subject of verb contradict.. 9-key used
as a qualificative adjective and means important. 10- wild means
licentious. 11- hold means consider. 12- and does not pretend, it
replaces story. 13-those who search, those being a demonstrative
pronoun is the subject of verb pretend. 14- dense means large, wide.
15-forsoth means by truth, indeed. 16-rathe means blooming. 17-that
it only tries, it replaces reason. 18- reason, wisdom and convictionare
the subject of verb are needing. 19- originate means germinate,

beget.20- to recognize = for recognizing. 21- for it, it replaces religion. 22-religion is the subject of verbs of will turn, come, does not pretend.23-signal means remarkable. 24-it happens, it being an impersonal pronoun is the subject of verbhappens. 25- rathe means blooming. 26-it is no matter, it being an impersonal pronoun is the subject of verb is.. 28- sland means point of view, opinion. 29- search in it, it replaces religion. 30-doctrineful means religious. 31-opinios is the subject of verbs pretend and has been confined.. 32- wont means custom. 33- wits means intellectuals. 34-lore means knowledge, belief. 35- taken is an adjective passed participle of notion..

No 83

Wise advice

I

You are a surly guy, have a temperament
Of owl that really makes the life hard and bitter
To your domestic1 and friendly circles. Better
Occasion for forming2 a bouquet of cognent
Virtues: the modesty, the patience, the kindness,
The morality, the sweetness, the hopefulness,
The will, the humility and good sentiment.

II

Do for others what you want that they do for you.
Do not do for others what you do not then want
That they do for you. These both advices so wont
Must be engaged in your mind and in your new
Heart so that you might always strew3 the happiness,
The charity, the harmony, the forgiveness,
The peace, the understanding round you, all are due.

III

Fortunes push most people to look for the comfort,
For a new life in forgetting things on-earth. Eh!
Poverty pushes others to turn every day
Their eyes through sky4. Moreover, we tend to comport
Ourselves as the good persons because we had thus

Accumulated in our lives the numerous
And long speeches of wisdom, of moral support

IV

Without ever trying hard to discipline
Our interior self and to armonize it
With the words that we have told. O my explicit
Friends! How many beautiful formulas quite keen5
Learned6. by heart and recited automatically
Without our minds are not present in them8! Surely
Hom many lies are there in our chaste lives so serene!

V

Indeed, it is not important of shedding tears
On my life. I do what is right, this is truly
On yourselves that you need to weep since your daily
Lives remain in the morality and fears.
The man always forget himself and he often
Seeks to weep on others, never on himself. Then
Let me remain honest in all hemispheres.

VI

As being father, this is an initiative
Of love. Being father, this is loving children
Before they love; this is loving without even
When they do not love you, prompt to forgive!
Do they deserve to be treated in enemy?
Of course, without a steady love who can truly
Teach a wisdom and forgiveness quite positive.

VII

I constantly know that this individual
Is my correct fellow and I have to forgive
Him, this is the law of charity. It must live
And reign among humanity and actual
Family. How long we do not feel transported
By gladness, by emotion and by exhorted
Gratitude when we show a love quite mutual.

VIII

A wise man is the one who makes himself very
Inaccessible to inopportune rumor;
He makes the effort of subduing his vigor
And his exterior senses, and specially
For dominating his tendencies in order
To take care of others. All people are eager
To go sky, no one will need to die truly.

1-domestic means family. 2-forming means cultivating. 3-strew means spread, scatter. 4-through the sky = through the sky for the hope. 5-keen means wsensitive. 6- learned is an adjective past participleof formulas. Recited is an adjective past participle of formulas. 8- are not present in them, them replaces formulas.

No 84

Virtue of charity

I

The fire of love that consumes the heart of a wise
Appears during his whole life. To clear1 what there is
Of deepness in his attitude, this is to seize
Or it is admirable to see2 that the size3
Of his charity is endless and created
By all his experiences quite repeated
In a conscience that does not share it to all guys.

II

O you who are bearer of love and of peace may
Avoid all what is contrary to the essence
Of charity, neither displeasing remarks. Whence
Your only presence and behavior must stay
As a leaver of fraternal love, of concord,
Of togetherness, of conscience and of accord,
Of common support and forgiveness in goodway4.

III

If you are a gentle person, your appeasing
Presence becomes a spring of joy. You will not tend
To camouflage your nice position as a grand
Peacemaker. What love in the heart of becoming
A wordly peacemaker! This is a mark of great

Charity. Happy are those who become the straight5
Peacemakers by sharing to others their saving6.

IV

One day you recognize who you are and you will
See your work. And what you donate is as a ray
Of light glimmering other gloomyand dark-way
Lives that you spread. The most precious and very leal7
Testimony is not to tell what God has done
For you, what you have done for the others. Whence shun
The self that is inside us and you will be real.

V

Charity is not only to make donation
Being the important part of it8. Approaching
Whoever by loving to help them becoming
Better is also a great act of oblation9;
Approaching them demands so many constant tries
And so much patience, and laborious applies.
There is no better life out ofeducation.

VI

Approaching others is a part so essential,
Provided that in contacting them you carry
In your heart the love, the peace and morality,
Reconciliation; you must be impartial.
Approaching others with an empty character
Without purpose, this is truly an improper
Work, this is a time quite very superficial10.

VII

Betraying the mission whose you have as human
So important, this is to deceive the entire
World, this is to fail to take the road that they hire
You, this is to negociate the love and the plan
Of peace with the conflicts. Before you just intend
To run in the tract of peace, you must understand
That the rapports of power are quite inhuman.

VIII

No one is personal in the life, each one needs
Another; each one has his way to express it.
The one has tendency of complaining the split,
The other brags; other tells nothing and exceeds11.
One of greatest charities is trying to pick
Up the wise messages of conscience very quick
That emanate the others with so many heeds12.

IX

For the moment, the best way of telling someone
That you esteem or you love is to just render13
His life easier in the little and greater
Things. Do not only search to rival or to shun,
But collarate with the sincerity. Then.
Having toward the other a sense more often
Rival is an act of wickedness or weapon.

X

Appreciating the other people in joining
Together at what they try hard to do the best
Is also an act of charity. Be modest
When someone has a conduct that is surprising

You and is irratingyou, do not let you go
To judge very fast, let you enter comme il faut17
In your inside conscience that is legal, fitting.

XI

In any situation, do not please to take
Someone in fault. Everybody makes mistakes and
Find themselves interioly guilty, unbland
And ready to defend themselves by any fake
Reason. The virtue of humility is then
To accept conscience such as it is, and often
To admit that it tells your faults or your mistake.
1-to clearing = for clearing. 2-see means observe. 3-size means
dimension. 4-good way means good sense. 5-straight means
right.6-saving does not take a s, because of rhyme. 7-leans mens
legal.8- part of it, it replaces charity. 9-oblations means charity.
10-superficial means insignificant in the improper sense. 11-exceeds
means excels. 12- heeds means attentions. 13-render means
make. 14- shun means avoid, keep away. 15-appreciating is the
subject of verb is. 16- a conduct is surprising, that being being a
relative pronoun of conduct is the subject of verbs is surprising
and is irrating. 17-comme il faut being an adverbial locution
means as it should be proper, fitting. 18-such as it is, it replaces
conscience. 19- admit that it tells, it replaces conscience.

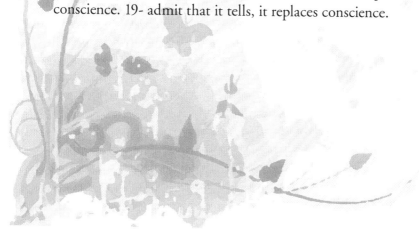

No 85

Looking for happiness

I

You who look for the happiness in the glory
In the vanity; you who look for a famous
Name; for obtaining it, do not admit to play
The evil. You see dying in the enormous
Worries so many seeming1 people in one day.
Life is not a chance. You strive yourselves truly2
To puff for masking your fear,
But your voice trembles as deer.
The death wears glove for taking
Us, it is not repressing
Without dozing off. And what then separates us
Has already lost its clearness, and its presence,
Its reality. You opine and you want to make
Me think4 that all black are alike in existence
By that forged Shem5 as an imperishable fake
That their dispectpects effect their disparate fuss6.

II

Consequently, you must bear a grudge at all that
Lessen the human values and human delight;
At all that conduce7 to make each one less wise,
Less confident or less prompt. With a certain light,
I will never accept that the morals will arise
With the slowness and the mistrust. Always the fat

360

Squirrels do not tolerate
Crawling of snake. Not too late,
Stop blaming what differs from
You; learn to fix with wisdom
What is wrong in you. A human assembly could
Be perfect if it calls for the use of many
Forms of activities, if it qualifies too
For opening certain forms of happiness. Would
You admit that no one can fail to do straightly
What the morality appoints each one to do.

III

Men are the same in all the times and in all places.
The story informs usthat nothing is new, strange.
Imagine that you are creating a fabric
Of human destiny with the objects of ange9
To make men glad in giving them peace, rest, civic.
Whatever be the content of your great bases
Of judgment9 of an object
Incorrect or quite correct,
It is important to go
Beyond it, if apropos
You wish to predicate existence of object.
You hope to just put and to this cynical10
Mode of argumentation by a strict meaning11
Of the conception of existence. Your ethical
Evidence does not teach that from our confounding
The illuions rise a logical, a sect.

IV

The worldwide counsuls yearly convene13 in meeting
About making the world on a better path. Then
Do you think at this time that powerful countries

Put themselves in the same condition that often
The poor countries find themselves? Never, no. Stories14
Of the race, of such ethnic groups really wanting15
To remain in the highest
Privilege cause the biggest
Malfeasances. I tell you
That they are still there quite true
By gain of this life. At each steps the poor countries
Take on the road of gain, they will see so much great
Certainty of gain, so much nothingness in what
They risk. This one that tries not to lose in the late
The true or normal reality then names brat16.
They17 let them18 know that the poorness comes by their glitches19.

V

I believe a little bit, no body can change
The world, but each one may then try to change oneself.
From where will it spring up, this new change? Not outside.
Learn to discover it in you; talk to yourself
About it22, and require it23 from you; do not slide24
Yourself. And under the blue sky, nothing is strange.
Expect and obtain it from
You.try again to become
Who are and who you will
Be; try to be clair until
In any consideration. There are really
So many admirable possibilities
In each person. Persuade yourself with your own
Understanding. Learn again to tell endlessly:
"This one depends on me! The abilities
Are in you, and particular in each one.

VI

To bring everwhere you can: the affluenc, joy,
Confidence, this becomes very soon your constraint
And the claim of your indispensable rapture;
As if from blkiss of others, you come to enjoy
Proper yours. Right now, I may tell you the restraint
Of all thingsthat stops the rapture inyour nature:
Shyness and discouragement,
Distrust and undiscernment,
Sel-satisfied undiscernment,
Self-satisfied case stories
Of invented poverties,
The vain thirst of unreal joy, and the divisions
Of parties, of classes, of races, of nations,
All those conduce to make from man an enemy
For the others, and the sowingof collisions26,
Denials, oppressions, and intimidations,
Behind each one there is a hidden reality.

VII

Now there are several monsters who deserve the fear
Than amount we have, this is partiality!
Monsters begotten by the fear: fear of night,
Fear of the light, fear of life, fear of assembly,
Fear of death, fear of God and Satan, fear of right.
And nevertheless not to be often here
Ridiculed transmits in you
The worst freedom. How sometime28
People of the slight propulsions
Thinkof having compulsions
That the world of utopian has defeated
And has applied to their convictions, and the fear
Of passing for the imaginary bodies

To eyes of sensed guys. As if all elevated
Progresses of humankinds were not due to dear
Utopia perforfemed by the genius.

VIII

As if the progresses of tomorrow are not
Made by the utopia of yesterday and
Today. Without the great idea of the progress,
The life is for us no price and is not quite planned.
Evevrything you have not done, everything you caress29
To do and you do not do, decrease you a lot.
The regret is the most vain
Occupationof profane
Elder. You most estimate
That the regrets bring you straight
To conviction. What is normal is to invent
Or to do something that is complete service
Of humanity. Invent for human being
Everything that you judge that it is a delice
To the progress. Whence mutual help is a thing
Of virtue, but it is also an enjoyment.
1-seeming means illusive. 2- you strive yourself truly = you truly
strive yourself.. 3- puff means make proud or conceited extravagantly.
4-think means believe. 5- Shem is the elder son Noah. 6- fuss
means declination. 7-conduces means leads. 8- ange means purity.
9-judgment means conception.10- cynical means negative, picking.
11meaning signification. 12-your ethical evidence does not teach
that from our confounding the illusions rise a logical, a sect = your
ethical evidence does not teach that the illusions rise a logical, a
sect fromour confounding. 13- convene means meet. 14-storie is
the subject of verb cause. 15-wanting = that want. 16-bvrat means
corrupted country. 17-they lket them know, they replaces powerful
countries. 18-they let them know them replaces poor counties.
19-glitches meansa malfunctions.20- from where will it spring upit

replaces change. 21- to discover it, it replaces change. 22-to talk to yourself about it, it replacesit replaces change. 23-and required it, it replaces change. 24-slide means neglect in the improper sense. 25-sowing means scattering. 26-collisions means conflicts in the improper sense.27- fear is the subject of verb transmits. 28- sometime is an adverb of time and means one day. 29- caress means embrace.

No 86

Discipline and self-esteem

I

Affirming your value is not an easy task.
Today, you believe that your worth and your self-back1
Depend on your conduct. Metaphorically,
You see yourself as an empty pot that you must be
Filled withyour achivements. The truth is that your worth
Is yoiur consciousness, your ability as mirth
To perceive and to experience. The value
Of human life is that it exists, it is true.

II

You have to learn to affirm yourself if you are
Disarming the critic. When critic has so far2
Been silenced, you need to fairly replace your voice
With a positive awareness of an own choice
Of your worth. The best way to disarm the critic
Is to render it useless. Take away its quick
Role and at last it will be silent. Disarming
Critic is the task of every human being.

III

Discipline is an instruction that corrects, molds
The mewntal faculties. The parents or households
Are as of instructorsand trainers, and they teach

Their children with so much skill being very rich
That people need to livein the world. Normally,
If the rules are predictable, their kids freely
Feel freely accepted as persons, even when their true
Behaviors are not acceptable and due.

IV

It is a mistake to think that children who are
Never disciplined or quite limited so far
May grow with the self-esteem. The children who raise
Without rule are assaults on self-esteem, they3 praise
To be dependentand achieveless, and often
Feel that they have less control over their world. Then
The rule is an assault on the self-pride. It may
Be the path of making a safe household quite gayt.

V

When you make everuything easy for the children
To behave well, their delf-esteem grow. And even
They learn to see themselves in a positive light,
And they feel successful to please you in the right
Way. Be surethat your expectations are conscious
And appropriate for the age your child. Thus
Having good hope for level of developmemt
Of the child avoids conflict and disappointment.

VI

When you know that a situation will be then
Difficult for your own children, do what often
You can help them to cope. Children are less ;likely
To be patient, pleasant flexible, specially
When they are tired and hungry. Your children are more
Likely to meet your expectations if encore

You clearly define what you thus mean by "be good"
At school or any place, you will be understood.

VII

Use every opportunity to compliment
And to reinforce "good conduct and effort". Plant
In them all the good manners. If they feel clearly
That they are partially successful already,
It will be easier for them to try harder
To get it right. Whence they can learn and grow gladder
With good self-esteem. Be a good role model then
In how you deal with your own strong feeling often.

VIII

Punishment is defined as enforcing order
And fairly implies external control over
A person by force or coercion. You have power
In the relationship with your child quite slower.
You are physically strong, more intelligent
And experienced. Your control reinforcement,
Children live in your house. Since your children depend
On you for support, approval, love, advice, hand.

IX

And feeling of wortjh, you have the immense power
To intimidate them and to force them slower
To obey. At this time how do you keep a good
Relationship when you correct them with mood,
Limit them and direct them? You do by using
The exact communication skills when dealing
With another person around conflicts; then
Your child may tremind you by yourself more often.

X

Neither how now you are nor how you use to be.
If your children have your negative quality,
You might be excessively sensitive to them.
As a responsible parent with sense of stem,
You should be careful not to fall inti the trap
Of focusing on the negative and flip-flap,
Comportments that a matter of the druther
Or something that your children have controlled over.

XI

For the most powerful tool you have as parent
To create good sel-esteem is the evident
Language that you use. The language of self-esteem
Is a language of description that you thus seem
To describe yet the comportment without judging
The child. In this matter, you are distinguishing
Between the worth of child and his or her conduct,

XII

On what you see and what you hear, this gives children
Accurate feedback about how they act often
And how their actions affect others. The private
Language of self-esteem is a language so straight
That shares something useful about yourself. You share
Your appreciation, your enjoyment, and your bare
Annoyance; you communicate your reason
For wanting something done, your beautiful season.
1-self-back meansself-pride.2-so far is an adverb. 3-they praise
to be, they replaces children ans is the subject of verbpraise
and feel. 4-light means enlightenment, edification, awareness,
understanding,. 5- having being a present participle is the subject of
verb avoids. 6-cope means subsist. 7-plant in them, them replaces

children.8-if they feel clearly, they replaces children. 9- that they are partially, they replaces children. 10-for them to try harder, them replaces children. 11-when they can learn, they replaces children. 12-reinforcement means resources in the improper sense. 13- hand means help. 14-stem means family. 16-describing = to describe. 17 pivate means personal.. 18- bare means simple.

No 87

Fraternal love

I

What is the point
Of making the union of religions,
If all the religions in all regions
Do not love other sects. What is the use
Of union in United Nations, news,
Conjoint and joint ......,
If there is no togetherness at base?
How many fractions among them that raise!
How many indifferences, quarrels,
Barriers, hatred, jealousy, scoundrels
Among the true
Members of United Nations, the same
Family, the same sector, the same name,
The same race and same continent, between
Religions of offbeat faiths, the same scene,
Between the due
Guys of diverse races, colors, countries!
There certain members in their duties,
In the cults feel uneasy, who are then
Freezing in the active meetings often
Decisive, and
Who has been truly frightened to see how
Their colleagues lied in the assemblies, now
Who remain cold and so indifferent

From each other and very arrogant.
No soul is grand.
Some people did not find in the meetings
Enough good will and enough welcomings,
Enough ruth and truth; others took other
Aimsthat will never make the life better
For the meager
Lands. They just discussed on what they never
Found an accord among them. Moreover,
What they came to support, this is only
Their friendly politics. As much as we
Love forever
Our brothers and we will show it, the life
Will be better on the earth, not with strife.
Let us put ourselves together and love
Those who are poor, and will see above
How we suppose
To attribute the conversatioin of heart;
The chang of heart is not to talk in part
About Buddha, Jesus and Mohammed.
It is in the deeds that we promoted.
We are so close
For showing our mutual love as lot.
We pretend to love God that we do not
See, this is a lie. The religious and
Governmental leaders quite very fanned
For uniting
Themselves to God that tey do not see,
We consciously support war that daily
Kills our brothers that we see, this is love.
How we could stop provocation above
Our availing.
It seems that the wars, conflicts, privations,
Poverties keep the United Nations

Alive; without them, this box will be closed.
That proves there are no people who disposed
Themselves to do
The right things. There is a fear through the world:
A fear of invasion, a fear of whorled
Exploitation, a fear of religions;
Those fears will push all the worldly regions
To build their true
Defenses. This is in vain that the great
United Nations will schedule private
Meetings if by coming in there is no
Open heart to each other, this seems a show.
The world desires
To do a pact of union, if leaders
Do not plan themselves in their nice manners
Of remaining so impermeable
To others; this nice pact will be able
To change the ires
In the hearts of actors inside the box.
Talking about the poverty as pox
That takes seat in the thirds lands and living
In it are two different things. Talking
About it is
To perceive it, living it is to see
It or to feel it. Having tendency
To change situation of poor countries
Must push counsuls to work on poverties
As a disease.
O counsuls of the world! Judge yourselves and
Let world know who you are: a worldwide band
Of elves or of criminals. Try to know
That the wishful peace can normally show
The love and wit.
O worldwide leaders! Permit to tell

You that the truth is in your mouths, so well
You shut yours up; the truth is in your hands,
You let it go; the truth is in your lands,
You stamp it.

1-conjoint is a qualificative adjective of association. 2-joint is a qualificative adjective of association. 3-the dots of suspension replace association. 4-among them, them replaces religions and Inited Nations. 5-name is written at the singular because of rhyme. 6-offbeat being a qualificative adjective of faiths means very different. 7-scene is written at the singular because of rhyme. 8-ruth means pity. 9-aims means resolutions. 10-meager means little. 11-strife means fight, conflict. 12- fanned being a qualificative adjective of leaders means enthusiastic, devoted. 13- availing means interest, advantage. 14- whorled means twisted. 15-regions means countries. 16-actors means worldwide diplomats. 17-box is a metaphor of United Nations. 18-takind and living being the present participles are the subjects of verb are. 19-pox is any of various disease marked by a rash on the skin. 20-living and talking are the subjects of verb are. 21-living in it, it replaces poverty. 22-about it is, it replaces poverty. 23-to perceive it, it replaces poverty. 24-living being a present participle is the subject of verb is. 25- living in it, it replaces poverty. 26- to see it, it replaces poverty. 27-to feel it, it replaces poverty. 28- wit means sagacity, wisdom. 29 so well is an adverb. 30-yoiurs replaces mouths.

No 88

Body and sexuality

I

All education must be
Inspired by a specific
Conception of man. Truly,
The religious and civic
Educations then will tend
To advocate the moral
Realization as stand
Of man through the natural
Development of his being and of aptness
Of the nature and of the mindwhose it is then
Enriched by morals. Religious broad-mindedness
Is deep-rooted in the matter of faith often.

II

It always gives a new light,
Reveals and unveils the high
Project of God on the right
Basic vocation of guy.
In the religious vision
Of man, a particular
Function in a strict mission
Is observed by regular
Body because this one contributes to reveal
The sense of the life and the human vocation.

The body thus reveals the man by essense, still
Expressesthe person who is a formation.

III

Thus the body is the first
Message of God to the man
As a sort of the head- first
Sacrament showed as a plan
That just persuatively
Transmits in the visible
World the mystery truly
Divine and invisible
Hidden by God since the eternity. Again,
A second signification is thus about
Theological nature. The body even
Contributes to reveal God, his love and his stout.

IV

Because it does manifest
The character of creature
Of the man and its modest
Dependence of mature
Fundamental gift that is
Gift of morality. Whence
The body, the more it sees
Itself secuous in a sense,
Expresses the perfect vocation of the man
To the reciprocity, and this is to say
To the love and to the mutual and pure plan;
This is the self-talent, talent of a good way.

V

At last the body reminds
One more time man and woman
To their valuable kinds
And their vocations often
To the fecundity, thus
As at a fundamental
Meaning of their secuous
Beings. And the sexual
Distinction that seems as a determination
Of the human being is a diversity,
But in the equality of conformation,
Of the dignity and of the morality!

VI

For example, the human
Person, by his intimate
Nature, requires a true plan
Of relationship of great
Change in the form implying
A great responsibility
Of love. The sexes being
Just are complementary,
Similar and dissimilar, and not the same,
But equal by the dignity and character.
They are equal for understanding, not with the blame,
Each other, diverse for completing each other.

VII

Whence the man and the woman
Just constitute two manners
By reason of which human

Creature obtains and offers
A participation then
Determined by the divine
Being; and they are even
Coinstituted with the fine
Picture of God and realize this vocation
Not only as individual person, but
Also as couple, as house of appreciation
And of love where there is not any place of slut.

VIII

Oriented by virtue
Of union and fecundity,
The married woman and due
Man participate many
A time in the love of God
By staying in the union
With him and in his whole nod.
Man must live in communion
With his wife. The presence of corruption darkens
The original virginity, render less
Easy to the man the perception of intense
Senses: to solve them becomes a task quite flawless.

IX

Deciphering them became
An ethical task, object
Of a complicated blame
Or feat trusted by correct
Men. For the discovering
Of nuptial significance
Of body will stop being
For them a ciear and good sense.

This significance will rest as a task given
To man by echo of gift inscribed in deep
Of human heart; as a distant echo hidden
Of natural virginity, it is not flip.

X

Indeed, this capacity
Of entire body being
At the same time augury.
Instrument and a suiting
Vocation often permits
To discover a dainty
Connection between habits
And decency of body
That is the concrete route through which the true virtues
Come to the man. The sexuality is then
Appealed to expressed the diverse vital values
To which the morals need to correspond often.

XI

Sexuality being
Surely oriented through
Interpersonal, living
Dialogues contributes too
To the full maturation
Of man in opening it
Straight for the self-donation
In a love very complete.
According to the facts, the sexuality
Being connected with the order of creature
That is the fecundity and the primary
Transmission of life: tis is law of the nature.

XII

Love and fecundity are
The significations and
The great values quite bizarre
Of sexuality planned
That are reciprocally
Called and cannot be even
Considered as enemy,
As alternative. And then
The equitable and affective life, proper
To the one and to the other sex, expresses
Itself about a characteristic manner
In the diverse states of life: union of spouses.

1-stand means plan of action. 2-it always gives a new light, it replaces moral realization. 3-project meane intention in the improper sense. 4-guy means person, human being. 5-body means corporeal structure. 6-formation means creation. 7-showed being an adjective past participle of sort means embraced, comprised. 8-persuatively means effectively. 9-hidden is an adjective pastparticiple of mystery. 10-stout means strength, energy. 11- because it does manifest, it replaces body. 12-valuable means constructive. 13-conformation means structure. 14-same means identical. 15-character means person. 16-they are equal for understanding, not with the blame each other = they atre equal for understanding each othernot with the blame. 17-diverse for completing each other = they are diverse for completing each other. 18-determined is an adjective past participle of participation. 19- divine Being means God. 20-many a time means often. 21- nod means acknowledgement. 22- correct means wise. 23- virginity means innocencity. 24- augury means sign. 25- dainty means important. 26- that is the correct route, that being a relativepronoun of connection is the subject of verb is. 27- interpersonal is a qualificative adjective of dialogues. 28-living is a qualificative adjective of dialogues. 29-primary means valuable. 30-life is the subject of verb expresses.